Praise for HOT ROD Activity Books

"This is the most comprehensive set of literacy activities I have seen in one book!" **- Dannah Fritz Co-Owner of Jacksonville Tutoring Specialists, Advanced Certified in Barton & Accredited IEW Instructor**

The Raven Remix Activity Book features a collection of cleverly crafted exercises for teaching syntax. Teachers and tutors can use this activity book directly in classroom or tutoring settings without needing to prepare a complicated series of lessons in advance. The Activity Book is organized, sequential, and closely tied to *The Raven Remix* content. The grammar and syntax exercises are challenging, straightforward, and scaffolded to deepen comprehension and written expression. *The Raven Remix Activity Book* is a gift to all teachers. - **Paula Moraine, M.Ed., teacher, tutor, and author of *Helping Students Take Control of Everyday Executive Functions: The Attention Fix*.**

"As an SLP, I highly recommend Dean's HOT ROD Activity Books to my colleagues! I love these books because they simultaneously target articulation, oral language, and literacy skills. It's a comprehensive tool that not only improves speech but also supports overall language development! This is a must-have for any SLP!" - **Ellen Cieszkiewicz Rigg, M.A. CCC-SLP, A/OGA**

"What a powerful tool for anyone supporting learners! The Comprehension section includes practical strategies to assist learners as they explore texts. Students' comprehension will be supported by using the PAGES framework to help them think critically about the text they're reading. This chapter also gives learners signal words and practice paragraphs to help determine what type of text they're reading. Students' skills and confidence will grow if they utilize these strategies." **-Jolene Gutierrez, M.L.S., author of *Too Much! An Overwhelming Day*, teacher/librarian at Denver Academy, a school for neurodivergent learners, including those with dyslexia**

The Raven Remix Activity Book
by
Carolee Dean, MS, CCC-SLP, CALT

based on

The Raven Remix:

A Mashup of Poe Titles

by Carolee Dean

Word Travel Press LLC - Littleton, CO

HOT ROD – **H**igher **O**rder **T**hinking
through the **R**eading **of** **D**ecodables

The Raven Remix
Activity Book
by Carolee Dean

based on

The Raven Remix:

A Mashup of Poe Titles

A HOT ROD Decodable Book

Level 3

Closed, Open, Consonant –le Syllables

Vowel Teams - ee, oo

Suffix –ed, -ing, -en

Find this chapter book and others on the website

https://www.wordtravelpress.com/shop

Find the Scope & Sequence for the Series at

www.wordtravelpress.com

Cover Art by Krista Weltner

Cover Design by Sierra Gondrez

Contents

INTRODUCTORY MATERIAL

ACTIVITY SECTIONS

Contents

Contents

Contents

About the Author

Direct questions or comments to:
info@wordtravelpress.com

Carolee Dean, MS, CCC-SLP, CALT is a board-certified speech-language pathologist and a dyslexia interventionist with 20 years of experience working in public schools. She is a former president of the Southwest Branch of the International Dyslexia Association, a Regional Representative for IDA, and a frequent speaker at educational conferences. Dean serves as an adjunct instructor in the Master's in Literacy and Special Education program at Providence College and is the author of *Story Frames for Teaching Literacy: Enhancing Student Learning Through the Power of Storytelling* (Paul H. Brookes Publishing Co., 2021).

Dean is also a children's author of award-winning young adult titles: *Comfort* (Houghton Mifflin), *Take Me There* (Simon Pulse: A Division and Simon and Schuster), a YALSA Quick Pick for Reluctant Readers, and *Forget Me Not* (Simon Pulse), a novel in verse

Dean has combined her love of children's literature and her passion for helping struggling readers to create the HOT ROD Series – **H**igher **O**rder **T**hinking through the **R**eading **of D**ecodables. The purpose of the series is to provide older struggling readers with meaningful text that connects to the curriculum. Because of her background in language development and speech-language pathology, each book is accompanied by activities to foster growth in all the components of reading as well as language development and articulation. For additional resources see the information on the next page.

HOT ROD - Higher Order Thinking through the Reading Of Decodables

Additional Resources

The chapter book, *The Raven Remix: A Mashup of Poe Titles* is a decodable chapter book for older students (grades 5-8 and above). It contains a decodable story poem based on Poe's classic poem "The Raven." It aligns with Level 3 of the HOT ROD Scope and Sequence, which includes the following syllable types:

> closed, open, and consonant –le, vowel teams ee, oo

The book also contains an extensive background section on the life and death of Edgar Allan Poe, including several theories about his mysterious death. The background information is not considered decodable, but each section has a word count and an overall grade level of 6.6 (sixth grade, mid year) as calculated by ATOS at https://www.renaissance.com/edword/atos/.

The Raven Remix: A Mashup of Poe Titles may be found on the STORE page at www.wordtravelpress.com. Watch the website for information about the audiobook coming soon.

The Raven Remix is also available online at Amazon, Barnes & Noble, or your favorite local bookstore. Simply go to your bookstore's website. When you get to the SEARCH option, type in the title of the book. Another option is to visit https://bookshop.org/.

Schools and Libraries may purchase books from Ingram in paperback, hardcover, and e-book formats. For information about bulk orders and purchase orders, contact info@wordtravelpress.com.

Although most activities can be completed without the chapter book, you will need the chapter book to get the full benefit of the material in this activity guide. The engaging illustrations provide students with the experience of reading a real book that may be sent home for reading fluency practice. If sending the book home, be sure to include a copy of the page that explains the Pair and Share Reading Strategy.

Digital Boom™ Learning Cards are available for a small additional fee. Some decks are free , including the first **Cognitive Flexibility Game**. Go to https://wow.boomlearning.com and explore **Store>Word Travel Press.** Check out the **Four in a Row Games: 8 Virtual Board Games** provide fun practice for closed, open, and consonant –le syllables as well as /s/ blends, /r/ blends, and /l/ blends.

Decodable Chapter Book

Digital Boom™ Learning Cards

Audio Book Coming Soon

Target Users

The chapter book, *The Raven Remix: A Mashup of Poe Titles* aligns with Level 3 of the HOT ROD Series- Higher Order Thinking through the Reading of Decodables. It was written primarily for students in grades 5 and up who still need work on decoding words that contain closed (short) vowels, open (long) vowels, final consonant –le, and vowels teams ee and oo. Consonant blends and suffix –ed are included. The emphasis is on two-syllable words. The story is appropriate for use with general education students as well.

This Activity Book includes word lists along with numerous activities that focus on the Components of Reading (COR) that support reading comprehension and writing. Go to www.wordtravelpress.com to find the Scope and Sequence of the series.

Information in the Background Section varies in difficulty with an overall reading level of 6.6 (grade 6 middle of the year) as measured by ATOS. Younger students and struggling readers may listen to the introduction and background information read aloud and read the story poem themselves with support.

Books from the HOT ROD Series can be used to supplement any reading program but were specifically designed to support Orton-Gillingham based instruction. Level 3 may contain more elements than are traditionally taught to beginning readers. That is because these stories and poems were designed as a review and consolidation of concepts. They are also intended for older readers who often have a higher sight word vocabulary than younger readers as well as more exposure to suffixes and prefixes. The decodable story may be used at any point after the concepts for Level 3 have been introduced. Students should understand the idea that the unstressed vowel in a multi-syllable words may sound like a schwa ("uh").

The chapter book and the activities in this guide were designed to reinforce the concepts outlined above.

Speech-Language Pathologists
16 Ways to Address Articulation of /r/, /s/ and /l/ using *The Raven Remix Activity Book*

An SLP can use the material in **The Raven Remix Activity Book** to work on goals in all the areas listed in the Components of Reading Overview. Many of the skills that make a student a good reader also promote strong oral language skills. However, since many SLPs focus on articulation and speech sound production, the activities listed below help to illustrate how students can work on the /s/,/r/, and /l/ sounds in a variety of contexts. In this way, SLPs can support numerous reading skills while working on speech goals. The emphasis is on two-syllable words, but many one-syllable words in the book also contain this pattern.

Word Level

Card Games may be played with one and two-syllable S, R, L words on flashcards (pp.41-52)

Four-in-a-Row Gameboards (p. 66-69) focus on initial S, R, L sounds and blends as well as final consonant –le.

Phonological Awareness incorporates initial sound deletion in S & R blends on p. 99-100, final L deletion on p. 101, and medial /r deletion on page 102.

Sound Tracks on p. 103, students move one letter tile at a time to create new words as spoken by the therapist. They must make the sound change where they hear the change. Lists include several S, R, L blends. A Free Boom™ Learning activity allows students to move digital letters.

WOW Vocabulary (p. 178-179) Make vocabulary foldables with a focus on S words.

Sentence Level

Dictation activities on (pp. 81-83) may be used to read sentences with S, R, L words.

Rhyme Time (p. 109) students identify rhymes in words with S, R, L blends and create sentences.

Cognitive Flexibility (p. 133) Sort words into categories. Several words include final L.

Morpho Mania #3 (pp. 149) explores words and sentences with prefix RE.

Morpho Mania #5 (pp. 151-154) students use a word matrix to create word sums using the base element SIST. Then they use the sums to complete sentences.

Morpho Mania #6 (pp. 156-160) same as #5 but using base element SPECT.

Sentence Construction: Compound Subjects and Predicates (p. 196) Each sentence includes at least one initial R blend word. **Independent and Dependent Clauses** (p. 204). Each sentence includes at least one initial S blend word.

Paragraph Level & Extended Text

What's My Text Type (pp.229-231) Students read paragraphs and use signal words to decide on the text type being used (description, sequence, compare/contrast, problem/solution, etc). They can identify words with target sounds in the paragraphs they read.

Discourse Level

Sentence Quest – (pp.220-221) Students create sentences from SPECT words and then use those words to create a story which they read aloud.

Story Frames Plot Analysis (pp. 225-226). Students retell the story from *The Raven Remix* using the Plot Analysis storyboard as a guide. Encourage them to incorporate target sounds in the words they choose.

Parroty Parody – (p. 253) Students create a story using a Parrot or other animal with an R sound.

Pair and Share Reading

Pair and Share Reading is a strategy incorporated in the HOT ROD series that *pairs* developing readers with proficient readers (educators, parents, peers) who *share* the literacy experience by reading the more challenging segments of a text aloud while the developing reader reads the portions that are targeted for their decoding level.

The reading partner may be a reading interventionist, speech-language pathologist, or other educator working 1:1 or in a small group with students. In the classroom, teachers can more strategically assign portions of books to be read aloud by students at very different reading levels. Teachers may also pair struggling readers with more advanced ones to work together as reading partners. In the Background Section of the chapter book, each paragraph has been analyzed for grade level.

The stories from the HOT ROD series are perfect for parents who want to support the reading instruction happening at school or other settings. The books can be sent home for additional reading practice or parents may incorporate them on their own in consultation with a teacher, therapist, or reading tutor.

Finally, homeschoolers may use books from the series along with the Pair and Share strategy to provide reading fluency practice and to introduce their children to content at or beyond their current reading level. In fact, exposure to rich content is at the heart of the strategy. The activities may be used to work on a variety of skills across age and ability levels.

For information about the Scope and Sequence of the HOT ROD series and to find additional titles, go to https://wordtravelpress.com/.

Chapter books will also be available soon as audiobooks. Check the website for details.

How to Use This Resource

Scope and Sequence - Look at the scope and sequence for Level 3 to make sure the story aligns with the student's current decoding skill level. If not, words that contain unfamiliar patterns should be pre-taught as learned words.

Practice Reading Target Words – Patterns for Level 3 include closed syllables - short vowels in the first syllable (**a** – *apple*, **e** – *velvet*, **i** – *insect*, **o** – *pocket*, **u** – *sudden*), open syllables – long vowels in the first syllable (**a** – *bacon*, **e** – *sequin*, **i** – *silent*, **o** – *bonus*, **u** – *mutant*), and consonant –le in the final syllable (*table, little, middle, pickle, puzzle, simple*). Students should also be familiar with concepts taught in Levels 1 and 2 such as a = /o/ after w (waffle) and double vowels **ee** (beetle) and **oo** (book). Practice the Target Word Lists to make sure the student is accurate 90% of the time before they read the story poem.

Learned Words - Learned words must be taught prior to reading either because they contain an irregular pattern or because they include a pattern that has not yet been taught. Use the Copy & Memorize strategy described later in this Activity Book as needed.

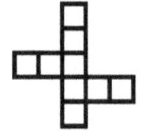

Pre-teach Vocabulary – Introduce unfamiliar vocabulary terms from the story before reading. Do the same for the vocabulary terms that go with the Background Information section.

Access Prior Knowledge – Before reading the story, share prior knowledge about Edgar Allan Poe as well as the genres of mystery, horror, and science fiction.

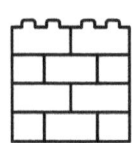

Work on Component Skills – Students often struggle with reading because of weakness in underlying skills other than or in addition to decoding. This resource is filled with supplementary materials to work on phonological awareness, cognitive flexibility, morphology, vocabulary, sentence structure, written language, and more. Choose the activities that best support your students' current needs.

Data Collection – See specific directions for calculating fluency. For activity pages, simply divide the number of correct responses by the total number of possible responses for a % correct. An approximate grade level has been provided for each section of the Background Information in the chapter book. Boom™ Cards may also be used for data collection.

Collaboration – Classroom teachers, reading interventionists, and speech-language pathologists may easily collaborate to explore different activities based on the same story content. Each professional may use the activities that support their goals and objectives for a particular student or classroom.

Reading Levels & Supports by Grade Level

Grades 6+ - Students with grade 5 skills and above should be able to read much of the book independently. Encourage them to study the key terms first. The information can then be used to work on written responses and higher-order thinking activities. Portions of the background section are written at a higher level, and students may need support with these.

Grades 5- Students may read the entire book with instructional support after vocabulary terms and names are formally introduced. They may need help parsing longer sentences and phrases. Question them often and have conversations to check for understanding. Pause and picture what is happening in the story and ask clarifying questions.

Grade 4- Students may practice reading the Target Words and Learned Words aloud. If accuracy is above 90%, they may read the decodable story with support after listening to the Introduction section. If accuracy is below 90%, they should continue practicing the target words and the sentences in the Dictation section until they can read them with ease, or they should listen to the story being read aloud. Introduce the concepts of visualizing and self-questioning. Pick and choose what Background Information sections to share based on what is age-appropriate and relevant to the curriculum.

Level 3 Decoding (Use with any grade)

Regardless of age or grade level, students working at decoding Level 3 of the HOT ROD Scope and Sequence (found at https://wordtravelpress.com) or a similar program should follow the steps below:

1. Practice reading the Target Words and Learned Words to 90% accuracy or higher.

2. Listen to an explanation of the Key Terms.

3. Listen to the Introduction read aloud. Pause and picture what is happening in the story. Practice self-questioning when information is confusing.

4. The student reads the Decodable Story Poem out loud to a reading partner.

5. Discuss the HOT TOPIC questions at the end of the chapter book.

6. Listen to the portions of the Background Information that are age - appropriate and relevant to the classroom or therapy objectives.

7. When completing various sections of the Activity Book, be aware of material that is not decodable based on syllable patterns that have not yet been taught and read those sections to the student as needed.

Copy and Memorize Strategy

Decodable books and stories use words based on syllable patterns that the student has been taught strategically and systematically, but they typically also contain some phonetically irregular words that cannot be decoded. These words only make up about 5-10% of the English language, but they occur frequently in books and in spoken language. Their use should be limited ideally to 5% of a text or less in decodable books. We call these words **Learned Words**, though other programs may use different terminology. They need to be pretaught before reading a decodable book using the steps below. In addition, if a text contains words that are regular but based on patterns that have not yet been introduced, they should be taught as learned words for the text to be considered decodable.

Say – Say the word out loud and have the student repeat it.

Copy – Have students copy the word from a model, naming each letter as they write it. End with saying the whole word out loud again. Start with near-point copying with the word next to where the student is writing. Evolve to far-point copying with the word on a whiteboard five or more feet away. They may also start with **tracing** the word that someone else has written and then make a copy next to it.

Check – Instruct the student to check to make sure they have copied the word correctly. If not, repeat steps one and two.

Study – Look at the parts of the word and determine what sounds are spelled in an unexpected way. Which sounds are regular for spelling?

Copy – Copy the word again. Start with saying the word out loud. Copy it naming each letter. Say the word again after it has been written.

Memorize – Cover the word and write it from memory. Tell students to name each letter as they write it and end by saying the whole word out loud again.

Check – Uncover the word and check for accuracy. If needed, repeat the steps.

Fluency and Accuracy

Repeated Readings – Reading a text multiple times aloud has been shown to increase fluency, speed, and accuracy (National Reading Panel, 2000). Many of the stories in the HOT ROD Series incorporate poetry which naturally lends itself to repeated readings. In addition, because HOT ROD books involve engaging and high-quality content, students are excited to circle back to these stories as their decoding skills improve when they can read the entire book independently.

Calculating Accuracy and identifying Miscues for Decodable Passages - While the student reads aloud from the decodable story poem in the book, tally errors. You may calculate a percent correct, but poetry cannot be assessed for grade level because of unconventional punctuation use. Track student errors by using a counter clicker or tally on a piece of paper by making hash marks. If you want to record more detailed information about types of errors, use the following code: SC= self-corrections, I = insertions, R = repetitions, O = omissions, S = substitutions, and D = delays of more than 2 seconds.

Reading Fluency for Grade Level Passages – The introduction and background information portions are not decodable, but they have been analyzed according to ATOS to calculate an approximate grade level. You may derive fluency scores based on grade-level expectations from the introductory and background sections. Each reading passage is calculated separately so that measures of reading fluency may be assessed as desired. ATOS uses a readability formula based on average sentence length, average word length, and word difficulty level. To find out more about ATOS, visit https://www.renaissance.com/edword/atos/.

Calculate Accuracy –
Total Words Per Section – Errors = Total Correct.
Total Correct ÷ Total Words Per Section   = % Correct
Timed Reading Samples - You may want to time reading speed and calculate the number of words read accurately per minute, but please discontinue this practice if the student rushes, becomes anxious, or begins to use old, ineffective strategies like guessing.

Prosody – To work on prosody (patterns of stressed and unstressed syllables) see the activity called *Feel the Beat.*

Reference: Eunice Kennedy Shriver National Institute of Child Health and Human Development, NIH, DHHS. (2000). Report of the National Reading Panel: Teaching Children to Read: Reports of the Subgroups (00-4754). Washington, DC: U.S. Government Printing Office.

Online Use

1. For online learning, mail the chapter book, *The Raven Remix: A Mashup of Poe Titles* to the student OR use the e-book version of the chapter book and share it using Screen Share. Permission is granted for tele-education purposes. Email Activity Book pages to the school or home or upload pages onto Google Classroom. Activity pages may be printed wherever the student is located.

2. Boom™ Cards may be used to play online games. Some Boom Cards are free, and some require an additional fee.

3. Check all links to any online resources to make sure they are still accessible and appropriate. Some sites such as YouTube contain ads and should be avoided or closely monitored depending on the setting.

4. You may display your PDFs for students using the SCREEN SHARE feature of Zoom. You may also display any pages of the Activity Book using a document camera. A cell phone may be used in place of a document camera. You may turn on the ANNOTATE feature of Zoom to type or write on the PDF to show students examples of how to construct written responses or add diacritical coding marks to words. It will not save as you scroll, but you may take a screenshot if desired. If you have Adobe Pro, students may type directly on the PDF in edit mode.

5. Via the SCREEN SHARE feature of Zoom, give students the ability to share their screen with you so you can see their written computer work. If they are using pencil and paper, they may hold up their work or use a document camera to share it. They may also complete work in Google Classroom.

6. Online games may be shared using SCREEN SHARE. Use caution if you give students REMOTE CONTROL access since they are basically taking over your screen. Some educators prefer the option of having students give them verbal directions while playing games. Never display your entire desktop using Screen Share.

7. Note that if the student is using a Chrome Book, the Remote-Control feature will likely not be available on Zoom.

Components of Reading & Writing Overview

Each icon below represents a reading and/or writing component addressed in the activities for that section. Brief overviews are provided here, and longer descriptions are provided when you get to that section.

Decoding, Articulation, Spelling, and the Alphabet **Articulation** – A special note to speech-language pathologists on page 12 tells how to use the information in this section and the rest of the book to work on the /s/, /r/, and /l/ sounds in t wo-syllable words. **Target Words and Learned Words** - Read the columns of words as a preview before reading the story. **Four-in-a-Row** – Students search for target words to fit a variety of patterns using 8 different gameboards. **Dictation** – Sentences in this section may be used for reading and spelling practice. **Alphabet Code Breakers** – Use flash cards to practice what comes next in the alphabet, then decipher secret messages by using an alphabet-based code.

Phonological Awareness: **Say It Again, Sam** - Students work on deletion by repeating words and leaving out sounds or syllables. **Sound Tracks-** Change one sound at a time to create new words and non-words. **Feel the Beat** – Underline stressed words in the poem and practice reading with prosody and stress. **Rhyme Time #1**– Circle rhymes, underline alliterations, and write a sentence containing an alliteration. Generate words to complete a poem following a pattern of stressed and unstressed syllables. **Rhyme Time #2-3** – Analyze the Rhyme Scheme of "The Raven." **Rhyme Time #4** – Create a Poem Parody.

Cognitive Flexibility: The activities in this section are based on category sorts and multiple classification tasks. Words are sorted according to sound as well as semantic categories. Digital Boom™ Cards are also available online.

Morphology: **Morpho Mania:** Explore Suffix **–ED, -EN,** Prefix **RE,** Latin Base Elements – **SPECT, SIST,** Greek combining form **GRAPH,** and the etymology of **PLUTO**. Eight different activities include sentence completion, matching games, and word matrices

Vocabulary and Semantics: Create **Vocabulary Foldables**. Play **Multiple Meaning Matchup**. Have fun with **Catty Idioms** and **Feline Phrases**. Explore vocabulary using **Context Clues** by reading information based on the background section of the chapter book and searching the surrounding sentences for clues to word meaning.

Components of Reading & Writing Overview (continued)

<u>Sentence Construction:</u> Fifteen different syntax activities help students to identify **complete/incomplete sentences, compound subjects and predicates, direct objects**, and the difference between **phrases and clauses**. WH- questions help students explore phrases and clauses that tell **when**, **where**, and **why** things are happening. The **Sentence Quest** activity builds on the base element **SPECT** from the morphology section, and **Hiding Whodunnit** has students build their own complex sentences.

<u>Plot Structure, Story Retells, & Summaries</u>: **Story Plot Analysis** – Students read the story poem and draw stick figures to represent the action. Then, they decide which elements go in each frame of the Storyboard. Finally, they use the storyboard to retell the story or write a summary.

<u>Comprehension</u>: **PAGES –** This strategy includes Picturing, Asking, Going Back (or Forward), Exploring, and Summarizing. **What's My Test Type?:** Use the Signal Words in the Text Type Guide to determine the text type being used in six different paragraphs. **Comprehension Questions -** Answer the open-ended questions either verbally or in writing. Practice answering in complete sentences by restating the question before providing an answer.
RACE Responses – Follow the directions to turn the short answers into complete RACE responses to Restate, Answer, Cite, and Explain.

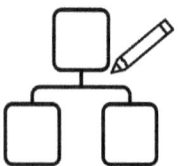

<u>Graphic Organizers for Paragraph & Essay Writing:</u> **Creature Features –** Write descriptions of the animals featured in various Poe stories. **Genre Gemstones** - Explore characteristics of the various genres written by Poe. **Balloon Brainstorm** – Compare and contrast gothic fiction and detective stories. **Cause of Death** – Discuss various theories about how Poe died. **High Five Writing** – Use the High Five template to brainstorm paragraphs based on writing prompts. **Compare/Contrast Essay** - Use the I+P+P+C directions to construct multi-paragraph essays.

<u>Create:</u> The highest level of Bloom's Taxonomy involves synthesizing what has been learned to create something new. This section contains a variety of fun and engaging creative writing prompts including **Scary Animals, Secret Codes, Parroty Parody,** and a reflection on **Tragedy and Resilience.**

HOT Topics – Explore this section to learn how the activities described above fit into the 24 categories of Bloom's Revised Taxonomy.

DECODING, ARTICULATION, SPELLING and the ALPHABET

INTRODUCTION

Articulation - Speech-language pathologists should reference page 12 for 16 Different Ways to Address Articulation of S, R, and L.

Target Words - Have students practice reading words BEFORE and AFTER reading the story. Compare performance. Use the word lists that follow and/or flashcards for decoding practice. Make two sets of cards to play Go Fish or the Memory Game. Some of these cards are available for free on Boom Cards.

Decoding - For students who need practice breaking words into syllables, instruct them to write out the word and put a bracket between any Consonant –le pattern and the rest of the word (example: ma[ple, ap[ple). Next, place a V under each vowel sound. Vowel teams like ee and oo are one sound and get one V. Place a C below each consonant sound. Digraphs like sh, th, ch are one sound and get one C. Split words according to these patterns: Closed = VC/CV (code the first vowel with a breve ‿. It will make its short sound. Open = V/CV (code the first vowel with a macron ‾. It will make its long sound. Words that don't follow these patterns or have stress in the second syllable are indicated on the word lists.

Learned Words – Have students practice these using the Copy and Memory Strategy.

Dictation: Sentences in the Dictation section may be used for reading and spelling practice at the sentence level.

Four-in-a-Row – Use a fun game format to practice finding words that contain closed, open, and consonant –le syllables. Games also address words with /s/, /r/, and /l/ blends.
Alphabet Code Breakers – Use flash cards to practice what letter comes next in the alphabet. Then, use an alphabet code to decipher secret messages.

Online resources, including free flash cards, may be found at https://wow.boomlearning.com. Explore Store>Word Travel Press.

Calculate Accuracy: While the student reads each target word aloud, tally errors. The number of words per column appears below that column. Subtract 1 point if they make an error and don't self-correct. Subtract half a point for self-corrections, repetitions, or delays of more than 2 seconds. Add up Errors. Subtract this total from the total number of words per column. This is the Total Number Correct. Divide the Total Number Correct by the Total Number Per Column = % correct.

21

Target Words
Closed First Syllable
Short ă, ĕ, ĭ, ŏ, ŭ

from *The Raven Remix*
by Carolee Dean

Word List #1– Practice these words either by reading the lists below or using the flashcards on the following pages. Some words are also available for free on Boom™ Cards. Bold indicates stress on a later syllable.

Patterns	Words	Total
Closed/short	**Vowel in first syllable**	
ă	ample, apple, ban**shee,** basket, cactus, fabric, fragment, jacket, mammal, mammoth, mandrill mantel, scramble	/13
ĕ	kettle, *met·al, pendulum, reddish, *rel·ish, settle, splendid, vellum, velvet	/8
ĭ	bitten, chicken, crimson, gibbon, griddle, hidden, insect, in**tent,** kitten, little, middle, pickle, picnic, riddle, simple, skillet, trinket, with**in**	/18
ŏ	blossom, common, contents, locket, oblong, pocket, socket	/7
ŭ	bumble, fumble, hubbub, jumble, muffin, nutmeg, plumcot, puzzle, ruckus, sudden, sullen	/11
a = ŏ	waffle, walnut	/2

*Students may need help dividing the syllables for *relish* and *metal* since they are closed but do not follow a vc/cv pattern. The pattern for these words is vc/v.

Target Words
Open First Syllable
Long ā, ē, ī, ō, ū
Vowel Teams ee, oo

from *The Raven Remix* by Carolee Dean

Word List #2– Practice these words either by reading the lists below or using the flashcards on the following pages.

Patterns	Words	Total
ā	bacon, ladle, table, maple, raven	/5
ē	be**gan**, equal, re**lax**, re**quest**, *se·cret, sequin	/6
ī	final, silent, spiral	/3
ō	bolo, bonus, broken, locust, woven opal, robot, topaz	/8
ū	gluten, mutant, strudel, Pluto, prudent, *pu·trid	/6
ee	ban**shee**, bee, beetle, beets, bumblebee, chimpan**zee**, creeping, deep, feeling, feet, fleet, free, glee, greens, greeted, Jeep, keeping, needed, needle, pedigree, peek, peered, queens, screeched, see, seen, seek, sheet, sleeping, reeling, teeth, three, tweet, week	/33
oo	book, foot, looked, nook, shook, wood, wooden	/7

*Students may need help dividing the syllables for *secret* and *putrid*. They do not follow a vc/cv or a v/cv syllable pattern. The pattern is v/ccv

Articulation Targets
L Words
from *The Raven Remix*
by Carolee Dean

Word List #3–Practice the words on the next few pages either by reading the lists below or using the flashcards on the following pages. They may be used to practice reading blends and/or by speech-language pathologists working with students with articulation challenges.

Patterns	Words	Total
	One-Syllable Words	
Initial L Blends	black, clam, fleet, glee, slammed, slipped	/6
	Two Syllable Words	
Initial L	ladle, landed, little, locket, locust	/5
Initial L Blends	blossom, clinging, flapping, flinging, gluten, plumcot, Pluto, slamming, sleeping, slinging, slipping, splendid	/12
Medial L	bolo, hulking, oblong, quelling, reeling, relax, relish, silent, sullen, telling, vellum, velvet, walnut, yelling	/14
Final Consonant - LE	ample, apple, beetle, bumble, fumble, jumble, kettle, ladle, little, maple, middle, needle, pickle, puzzle, riddle, scramble, settle, simple, table, waffle	/20
More Final L words	equal, final, mammal, mandrill, mantel, metal, opal, spiral, strudel	/9

Articulation Target Words
S & R
from *The Raven Remix*
by Carolee Dean

Word List #3–Practice these words either by reading the lists below or using the flashcards on the following pages.

Patterns	Words	Total
One-Syllable Words		
Initial S Blends	scan, script, skin, skip, skull, slipped, snack, spent, spot, stash, stock, stop, strong, swung	/14
Final S Blends	ask, blast, cask, chest, fast, gust, last, lost, mask, mist, must, next, past, pest, quest, twist, vest	/17
Initial R Blends	brat, crashed, drink, drop, free, grill, print, script, spring, three	/9
Two-Syllable Words		
Initial S	secret, settle, sequined, silent, simple, socket, sudden	/7
Initial S Blends	scramble, scratching, skillet, skipping, slamming, sleeping, slinging, slipping snacking, spiral, splendid, squinted, stacking, standing, stepping, stinging, stopping, strudel, stunning, swinging	/20
Initial R	racking, rapping, raven, reddish, reeling, relax, relish, request, resting riddle, ringing, robot, ruckus	/13
Initial R Blends	broken, crashing, creeping, crested, drifted, grabbing, greeted, grinned, grunted, pricking, printed, screeched, sprinted	/13

Suffix -ing Words

from *The Raven Remix*
by Carolee Dean

Word List #3–Practice these words either by reading the lists below or using the flashcards on the following pages. If students need practice decoding these words, instruct them to box off the suffix –ing and cross out any silent doubled letters before they analyze the rest of the word.

Patterns	Words	Total
No Change	beeping, bumping, clinging, creeping dinging, feeling, flinging, hatching, hulking, hunching, keeping, packing pinging, pricking, pumping, racking, reeling, resting, ringing, scratching, singing, sleeping, slinging, snatching, standing, stinging, swinging testing, thumping, wishing	/30
Doubling Rule	flapping, grabbing, hissing, missing, napping, rapping, shopping, sitting, skipping, stopping, stunning, tapping, telling, topping	/14
3 – syllable words	com**pel**ling, dis**miss**ing, dis**tress**ing In**sist**ing, up**set**ting, re**gret**ting	/6

Not a suffix –ing word: cunning
3-syllable words not listed elsewhere: chimpan**zee,** ped·i·gree

Bold indicates syllable stress on a location other than the first syllable.

Suffix -ed Words

from *The Raven Remix*
by Carolee Dean

Word List #3–Practice these words either by reading the lists below or using the flashcards on the following pages.

Patterns	Words	Total
-ed = /d/	grabbed, grinned, filled, happened, peered, penned, sequined, slammed, stunned, quelled, yelled	/11
-ed = /t/	chopped, clapped, crashed, etched, flapped, locked, looked, passed, picked, screeched. sketched, slipped, snacked, stacked, stepped, stopped stuffed, washed	/18
-ed = /ed/	crested, dented, drifted, ended, greeted, grunted, landed, needed, nested, pitted, printed, sprinted, squinted, tufted	/14

See the morphology section for an activity sorting these words according to the final sound.

The words above could also be sorted according to whether or not the doubling rule was used or by number of syllables, but the focus on this activity is on the final sound. Point out to students how adding /ed/ adds another syllable to the baseword.

Learned Words
from *The Raven Remix*
by Carolee Dean

LEARNED WORDS – Ask students to read the Learned Words list below or use the flashcards. Make a list of words they do not easily recognize and teach them according to the Copy and Memorize procedure. These words are considered "Learned Words" because they must be "learned" by heart either because:

1) They do not follow regular spelling patterns.
2) They are regular but their patterns have not yet been introduced.

Learned Words (Irregular)	Learned Words (Not Yet Introduced)
are	by
don't	for
eye	my
into	or
of	out
once	*ped-i-gree
there	
to	/6
was	
where	
were	
you	
some-thing	
/13	

pedigree contains a "misbehaving i" making the schwa sound which students will learn about later in the scope and sequence.

Word Cards

from *The Raven Remix*
by Carolee Dean

Flash Cards – Words on the following pages may be turned into flashcards by cutting them out and gluing them onto index cards OR you may use the card templates and copy them on cardstock before gluing. Make two copies to play card games like Go Fish or the Memory Game. Many of the flashcards are also available for FREE online as Boom Cards at https://wow.boomlearning.com. Explore Store>Word Travel Press.

Go Fish – Make a deck of 52 cards by choosing 26 target words. Make two copies of each word and glue the words onto index cards or card stock.
1. Shuffle the cards.
2. Each player receives 7 cards.
3. The rest of the deck is placed face-down on the table.
4. During a turn, a player asks another player for a specific word in their hand. If the second player has the card, they must give it to the first player. That player places the pair face up in front of them and gets a second turn.
5. If the second player does not have that card, they say, "Go Fish," and the first player must choose a card from the deck.
6. The game is over when one player runs out of cards.
7. The winner is the person who has the most pairs of cards.

The Memory Game – Make a deck of 12 cards by choosing 6 target words. Make two copies of each word and glue the words onto index cards or card stock. (Note: Increase the number of cards in increments if the student can handle more cards).
1. Shuffle the cards and place them face down on the table.
2. Each player takes turns turning over 2 cards at a time and reading the words on the cards. If the cards match, the player gets to keep those cards. Do NOT rearrange the remaining cards.
3. The game ends when there are no cards left.
4. The winner is the person who has the most pairs of cards.

Card Template

Word Cards /ă/

from *The Raven Remix*
by Carolee Dean

ample	jacket
apple	mammal
banshee	mammoth
basket	mandrill
cactus	mantel
fabric	scramble
fragment	

Word Cards /ĕ/

from *The Raven Remix*
by Carolee Dean

kettle

vellum

met•al

velvet

pendulum

reddish

rel•ish

settle

splendid

Word Cards /ĭ/
from *The Raven Remix*
by Carolee Dean

bitten	intent
chicken	kitten
crimson	little
gibbon	middle
griddle	pickle
hidden	picnic
insect	riddle

Word Cards /ĭ/ & /ŏ/
from *The Raven Remix*
by Carolee Dean

/ĭ/	common
simple	contents
skillet	locket
trinket	oblong
within	pocket
/ŏ/	socket
blossom	

bumble	puzzle
fumble	ruckus
hubbub	sudden
jumble	sullen
muffin	
nutmeg	
plumcot	

Word Cards /ā/ & /ē/

from *The Raven Remix*
by Carolee Dean

/ā/	/ē/
bacon	began
ladle	equal
table	relax
maple	request
raven	secret
	sequin

Word Cards and /ī/ & /ō/
from *The Raven Remix*
by Carolee Dean

/ī/	broken
final	locust
silent	woven
spiral	opal
/ō/	robot
bolo	topaz
bonus	

Word Cards /ū/ & /oo/
from *The Raven Remix*
by Carolee Dean

/ū/	/oo/
gluten	book
mutant	foot
strudel	looked
Pluto	nook
prudent	shook
putrid	wooden

Word Cards /ee/
from *The Raven Remix*
by Carolee Dean

banshee	feet
bee	fleet
beetle	free
beets	glee
creeping	greens
deep	greeted
feeling	Jeep

Word Cards /ee/

from *The Raven Remix*
by Carolee Dean

keeping	seen
needed	seek
needle	sheet
peek	teeth
peered	three
queens	tweet
screeched	week

One-syllable Initial S Blend Word Cards

from *The Raven Remix*
by Carolee Dean

scan	spent
script	spot
skin	stash
skip	stock
skull	stop
slipped	strong
snack	swung

One-syllable Final S Blend Word Cards
from *The Raven Remix*
by Carolee Dean

ask	lost
blast	mask
cask	mist
chest	must
fast	next
gust	past
last	pest

One-syllable S & R Blend Word Cards

from *The Raven Remix*
by Carolee Dean

quest	drop
twist	free
vest	grill
/r/ words	print
brat	script
crashed	spring
drink	three

Two-Syllable Initial S Word Cards
from *The Raven Remix*
by Carolee Dean

Initial S	sudden
secret	**Initial S Blends**
settle	scramble
sequined	scratching
silent	skillet
simple	skipping
socket	slamming

Two-Syllable Initial S Blend Word Cards

from *The Raven Remix*
by Carolee Dean

stacking

sleeping

slinging

slipping

snacking

spiral

splendid

squinted

standing

stepping

stinging

stopping

strudel

stunning

swinging

Two-Syllable Initial R Word Cards

from *The Raven Remix*
by Carolee Dean

R	relish
racking	request
rapping	resting
raven	riddle
reddish	ringing
reeling	robot
relax	ruckus

Two-Syllable Initial R Blend Word Cards

from *The Raven Remix*
by Carolee Dean

R Blend	greeted
broken	grinned
crashing	grunted
creeping	pricking
crested	printed
drifted	screeched
grabbing	sprinted

One & Two-Syllable Initial L Word Cards

from *The Raven Remix*
by Carolee Dean

One-Syllable Initial L Blends	Two-Syllable Initial L
black	ladle
clam	landed
fleet	little
glee	locket
slammed	locust
slipped	

Two-Syllable Initial L Blend Word Cards
from *The Raven Remix*
by Carolee Dean

blossom	slamming
clinging	sleeping
flapping	slinging
flinging	slipping
gluten	splendid
plumcot	
Pluto	

Two-Syllable Medial L Word Cards
from *The Raven Remix*
by Carolee Dean

bolo	silent
hulking	sullen
oblong	telling
quelling	vellum
reeling	velvet
relax	walnut
relish	yelling

Two-Syllable L – Final consonant-le Cards

ample

apple

beetle

bumble

fumble

jumble

kettle

ladle

little

maple

middle

needle

pickle

puzzle

riddle

Two-Syllable – Final Consonant –le Cards

scramble

settle

simple

table

waffle

More Final L words

equal

final

mammal

mandrill

mantel

metal

opal

spiral

strudel

Suffix -ed = /d/ Word Cards
from *The Raven Remix*
by Carolee Dean

grabbed

slammed

grinned

stunned

filled

quelled

happened

yelled

peered

penned

sequined

Suffix -ed = /t/ Word Cards
from *The Raven Remix*
by Carolee Dean

chopped	passed
clapped	picked
crashed	screeched
etched	slipped
flapped	snacked
locked	stacked
looked	stepped

Suffix -ed = /t/ Word Cards

from *The Raven Remix*
by Carolee Dean

stopped

stuffed

washed

55

Suffix -ed /ed/
Word Cards

from *The Raven Remix*
by Carolee Dean

needed

crested

nested

dented

pitted

drifted

printed

ended

sprinted

greeted

squinted

grunted

tufted

landed

Suffix -ing Word Cards
No change in base word

from *The Raven Remix*
by Carolee Dean

beeping	hatching
bumping	hulking
clinging	hunching
creeping	keeping
dinging	packing
feeling	pinging
flinging	pricking

Suffix -ing Word Cards - No change in base word

pumping	sleeping
racking	slinging
reeling	snatching
resting	standing
ringing	stinging
scratching	swinging
singing	testing
thumping	wishing

Suffix -ing Word Cards
Doubling Rule

from *The Raven Remix*
by Carolee Dean

flapping	sitting
grabbing	skipping
hissing	stopping
missing	stunning
napping	tapping
rapping	telling
shopping	topping

Word Cards
3-Syllable

from *The Raven Remix*
by Carolee Dean

bumblebee

chimpan**zee**

com**pell**ing

dis**miss**ing

dis**tress**ing

in**sist**ing

up**sett**ing

re**grett**ing

Learned Words – Irregular Words

from *The Raven Remix*
by Carolee Dean

Directions: If the student does not know these words, teach them as Learned Words using the Strategy of Trace, Copy, Memory.

are	there
don't	to
eye	was
into	where
of	were
once	you

Learned Words – Patterns Not Yet Learned

from *The Raven Remix*
by Carolee Dean

Directions: If the student does not know these words, teach them as Learned Words using the Strategy of Trace, Copy, Memory. The ones with * also appear in the target word lists.

by

for

my

or

out

ped-i-gree

FOUR-IN-A-ROW GAMES DIRECTIONS

PRINTED GAME BOARDS DIRECTIONS

For virtual play, use the Boom Card version (sold separately) and toggle between the game and virtual dice.

Print the game boards and laminate.

Print and cut out the game pieces. Each player chooses a color.

Roll dice (not included) or use virtual dice.

SEE THE DICE GUIDE

Choose a word that contains the target sound. Read it out loud. Place your game piece on the word.

The player who gets 4 in a row first is the winner.

©2023 WORD TRAVEL PRESS LLC

See the Downloads section near the end of the Activity Book for directions on how to download and print the full-color gameboards and access the virtual dice.

A digital game version is available at Boom™ Learning for a small additional fee.

FOUR-IN-A-ROW-GAMES
Dice Guides
Based on *The Raven Remix: A Mashup of Poe Titles* by Carolee Dean

Directions: Copy or print the Dice Guides in color from the online resources. Use the Dice Guides for the 4-in-a-Row Games.

Digital Gameboards are available on Boom™ Learning
Digital Dice may be found on the online resources page.

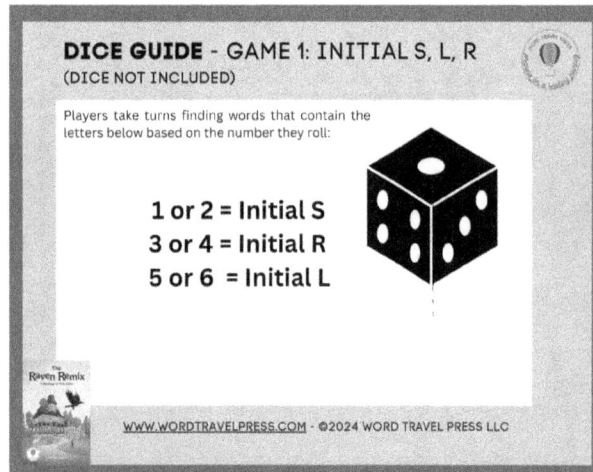

DICE GUIDE - GAME 1: INITIAL S, L, R
(DICE NOT INCLUDED)

Players take turns finding words that contain the letters below based on the number they roll:

1 or 2 = Initial S
3 or 4 = Initial R
5 or 6 = Initial L

WWW.WORDTRAVELPRESS.COM - ©2024 WORD TRAVEL PRESS LLC

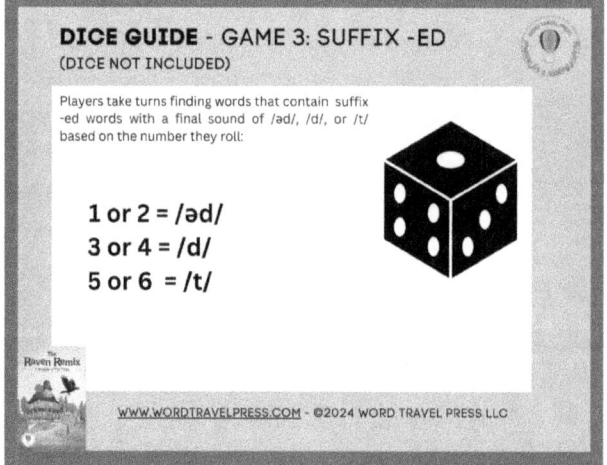

DICE GUIDE - GAME 3: SUFFIX -ED
(DICE NOT INCLUDED)

Players take turns finding words that contain suffix -ed words with a final sound of /əd/, /d/, or /t/ based on the number they roll:

1 or 2 = /əd/
3 or 4 = /d/
5 or 6 = /t/

WWW.WORDTRAVELPRESS.COM - ©2024 WORD TRAVEL PRESS LLC

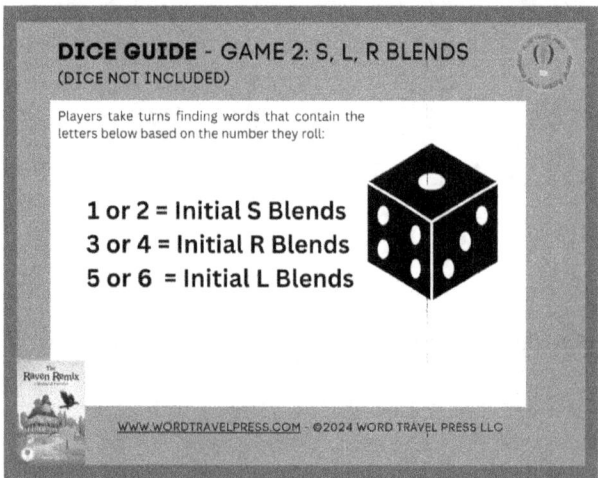

DICE GUIDE - GAME 2: S, L, R BLENDS
(DICE NOT INCLUDED)

Players take turns finding words that contain the letters below based on the number they roll:

1 or 2 = Initial S Blends
3 or 4 = Initial R Blends
5 or 6 = Initial L Blends

WWW.WORDTRAVELPRESS.COM - ©2024 WORD TRAVEL PRESS LLC

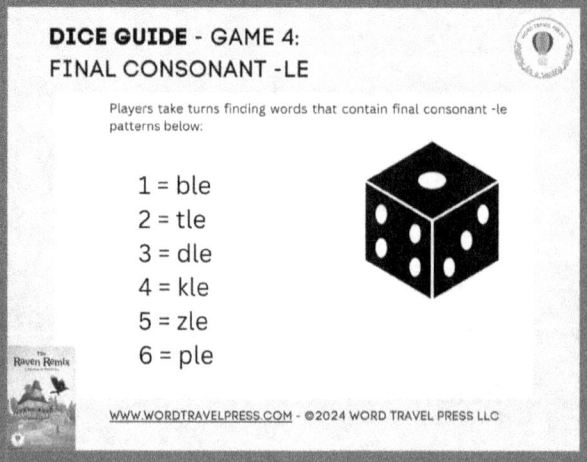

DICE GUIDE - GAME 4:
FINAL CONSONANT -LE

Players take turns finding words that contain final consonant -le patterns below:

1 = ble
2 = tle
3 = dle
4 = kle
5 = zle
6 = ple

WWW.WORDTRAVELPRESS.COM - ©2024 WORD TRAVEL PRESS LLC

FOUR-IN-A-ROW-GAMES
Dice Guides

Based on *The Raven Remix: A Mashup of Poe Titles*
by Carolee Dean

Directions: Copy or print the Dice Guides in color from the online resources. Use the Dice Guides for the 4-in-a-Row Games.

Digital Dice Guides and Gameboards are available on Boom™ Learning.

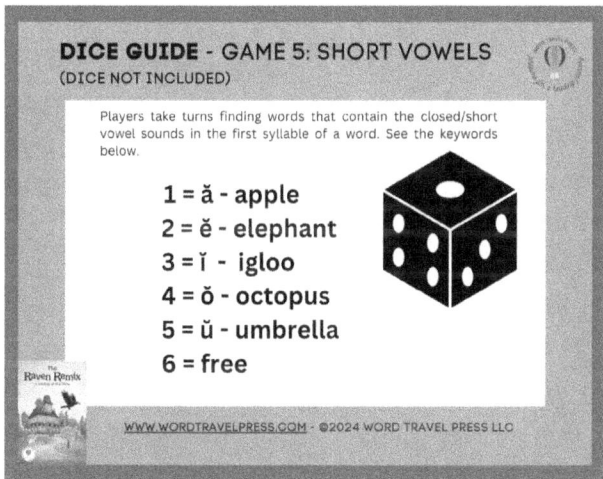

DICE GUIDE - GAME 5: SHORT VOWELS
(DICE NOT INCLUDED)

Players take turns finding words that contain the closed/short vowel sounds in the first syllable of a word. See the keywords below.

1 = ă - apple
2 = ĕ - elephant
3 = ĭ - igloo
4 = ŏ - octopus
5 = ŭ - umbrella
6 = free

WWW.WORDTRAVELPRESS.COM ©2024 WORD TRAVEL PRESS LLC

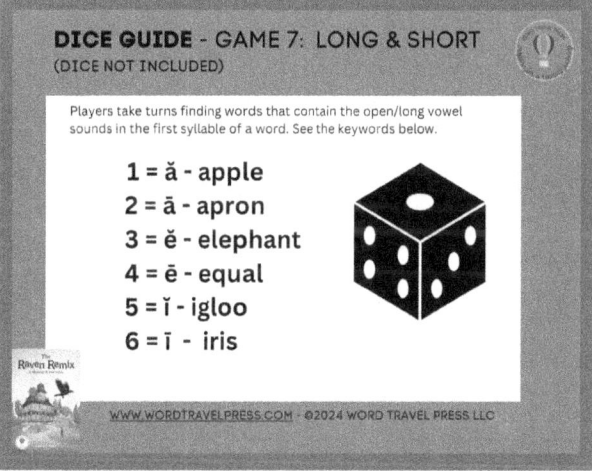

DICE GUIDE - GAME 7: LONG & SHORT
(DICE NOT INCLUDED)

Players take turns finding words that contain the open/long vowel sounds in the first syllable of a word. See the keywords below.

1 = ă - apple
2 = ā - apron
3 = ĕ - elephant
4 = ē - equal
5 = ĭ - igloo
6 = ī - iris

WWW.WORDTRAVELPRESS.COM ©2024 WORD TRAVEL PRESS LLC

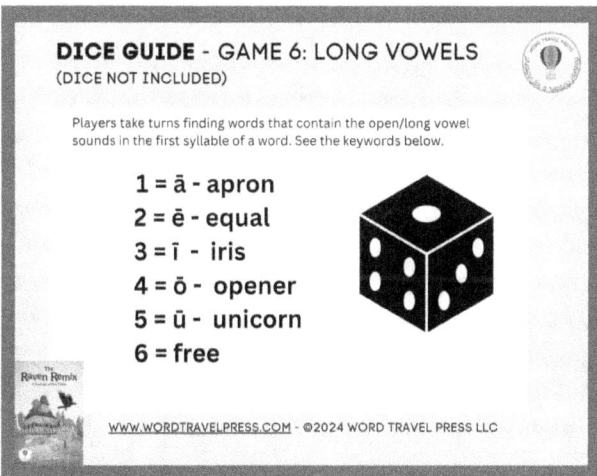

DICE GUIDE - GAME 6: LONG VOWELS
(DICE NOT INCLUDED)

Players take turns finding words that contain the open/long vowel sounds in the first syllable of a word. See the keywords below.

1 = ā - apron
2 = ē - equal
3 = ī - iris
4 = ō - opener
5 = ū - unicorn
6 = free

WWW.WORDTRAVELPRESS.COM · ©2024 WORD TRAVEL PRESS LLC

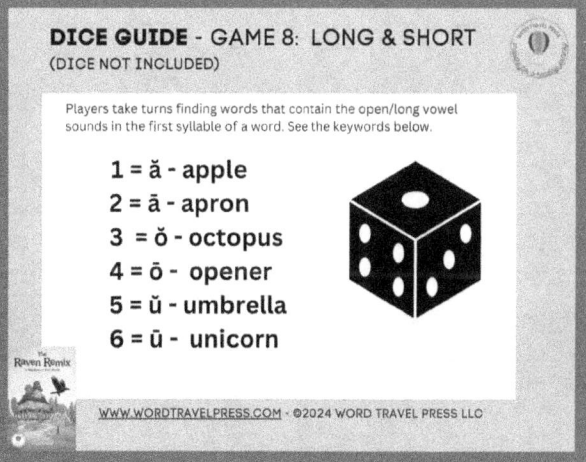

DICE GUIDE - GAME 8: LONG & SHORT
(DICE NOT INCLUDED)

Players take turns finding words that contain the open/long vowel sounds in the first syllable of a word. See the keywords below.

1 = ă - apple
2 = ā - apron
3 = ŏ - octopus
4 = ō - opener
5 = ŭ - umbrella
6 = ū - unicorn

WWW.WORDTRAVELPRESS.COM · ©2024 WORD TRAVEL PRESS LLC

Game 1: R, L, S - Initial Sounds
1-2 = S , 3-4 = R , 5-6 = L

relish	ladle	locking	silent	settle	raven
little	resting	socket	sudden	reddish	landed
sullen	secret	ringing	riddle	looking	locket
sequin	sadden	robot	reeling	locust	letting
lifting	ruckus	singing	landed	racking	simple

The Raven Remix
A Mashup of Poe Titles

Game 2: R, L, S - Initial Blends

1-2 = S Blends,   3-4 = R Blends,   5-6 = L Blends

skillet	greeted	flinging	spiral	broken	blossom
gluten	snacking	grabbing	Pluto	squinted	crashing
blending	plumcot	stacking	printed	crested	standing
swinging	pricking	flapping	stinging	drifted	clapping
flipping	printed	grinning	clinging	stopping	skipping

The Raven Remix
A Mashup of Poe Titles

Game 3: Suffix -ed:

1-2 = /ed/, 3-4 = /d/, 4-5 = /t/

grabbed	yelled	clapped	stacked	stuffed	looked
tufted	grinned	quelled	crashed	picked	washed
ended	printed	filled	stunned	etched	passed
dented	landed	pitted	peered	slammed	locked
crested	drifted	needed	nested	penned	sequined

The Raven Remix
A Mashup of Poe Tales

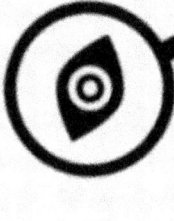

Game 4: Final Consonant -le

1 = ble, 2 = tle, 3 = dle, 4 = kle, 5 = zle, 6 = ple

pickle	beetle	dazzle	ladle	simple	jumble
kettle	middle	buckle	table	fizzle	apple
needle	drizzle	maple	bumble	prickle	settle
fumble	sample	little	speckle	riddle	puzzle
scramble	fiddle	ample	sizzle	cattle	cackle

Game 5: Short Vowel in the First Syllable
1 = ă, 2 = ĕ, 3 = ĭ, 4 = ŏ, 5 = ŭ, 6 = FREE

ample	kettle	chicken	blossom	jumble	sullen
fragment	mammal	reddish	crimson	common	plumcot
velvet	socket	basket	settle	gibbon	contents
hidden	pocket	bumble	cactus	splendid	griddle
insect	oblong	fumble	hubbub	fabric	vellum

The Raven Remix
A Mashup of Poe Tales

Game 6: Long Vowel in the First Syllable
1 = ā, 2 = ē, 3 = ī, 4 = ō, 5 = ū, 6 = FREE

bacon	even	final	bolo	pluto	putrid
staple	ladle	equal	silent	bonus	prudent
sequin	opal	table	refund	spiral	broken
idle	woven	mutant	maple	secret	siren
tribal	locust	gluten	strudel	raven	secret

WWW.WORDTRAVELPRESS.COM - ©2024 WORD TRAVEL PRESS LLC

Game 7: Long and Short Vowels in the First Syllable
1 = ă, 2 = ā, 3 = ĕ, 4 = ē, 5 = ĭ, 6 = ī

cradle	candle	sequin	metal	riddle	rival
defect	basil	saddle	demon	relish	bison
dentist	kitten	fatal	mammal	hero	fennel
denim	wiggle	pilot	radon	mammoth	evil
pickle	skillet	iris	lilac	label	scramble

Game 8: Long and Short Vowels in the First Syllable
1 = ă, 2 = ā, 3 = ŏ, 4 = ō, 5 = ŭ, 6 = ū

ruckus	topaz	focus	gobble	vacant	mandrill
noble	open	goblet	stable	mantel	coffee
robot	bonbon	staple	jacket	sudden	muffin
rocket	cable	basket	human	pupil	puzzle
fable	apple	student	bugle	music	juggle

WWW.WORDTRAVELPRESS.COM - ©2024 WORD TRAVEL PRESS LLC

The Raven Remix
A Mashup of Poe Titles

Download the PDF. Print. Cut out the game pieces.

CUT OUT THE GAME PIECES.

WWW.WORDTRAVELPRESS.COM - ©WORD TRAVEL PRESS LLC

Download the PDF. Print. Cut out the game pieces.

CUT OUT THE GAME PIECES.

 # DICTATION

/ă/ Words

based on *The Raven Remix*
by Carolee Dean

Directions: The following target words have short a in the first syllable. These sentences may be used for dictation, spelling, articulation, and/or reading practice. Questions are included so that students can practice final punctuation more deliberately. A digital version is available at Boom™ Learning for an additional fee.

Word	Sentence
1. ample	He had ample snacks.
2. apple	Is that apple red or green?
3. basket	The basket had rings in it.
4. cactus	Can you snack on cactus?
5. fabric	That fabric is soft.
6. fragment	Is that a fragment of cloth?
7. mammal	Is a cat a mammal?
8. mammoth	Is a mammoth big or little?
9. mandrill	Is a mandrill a chimp?
10. jacket	He had on a jacket.

/10

 # DICTATION

/ĕ/ Words

based on *The Raven Remix*
by Carolee Dean

Directions: The following sentences may be used for dictation, spelling, articulation, and/or reading practice. A digital version is available at Boom™ Learning for an additional fee.

Word	Sentence
1. kettle	Is it in the kettle?
2. nesting	Is it nesting on the shelf?
3. pendulum	Did the pendulum swing?
4. reddish	The mammal had reddish skin.
5. resting	Is the rat resting?
6. settle	We will settle on a plan.
7. splendid	The chest had splendid things in it.
8. testing	He had a long week of testing.
9. vellum	Is the bug on the sheet of vellum?
10. velvet	Is the vest velvet or silk? /10

* At this level, the student should have already been introduced to the concept of suffix -ing

DICTATION

/ĭ/ Words

based on *The Raven Remix*
by Carolee Dean

Directions: The following sentences may be used for dictation, spelling, articulation, and/or reading practice. A digital version is available at Boom™ Learning for an additional fee.

Word	Sentence
1. gibbon	Is a gibbon a chimp?
2. griddle	A griddle can be hot.
3. insect	Did the insect sting him?
4. kitten	Did the cat have kittens?
5. little	A kitten is a little cat.
6. middle	Is that a vest in the middle?
7. pickle	Is the pickle sweet?
8. simple	It is a simple plan.
9. skillet	He hit the bug with the skillet.
10. trinket	Did the chest have a trinket in it?

/10

DICTATION

/ŏ/ and /ŭ/ WORDS

based on *The Raven Remix*
by Carolee Dean

Directions: The following sentences may be used for dictation, spelling, articulation, and/or reading practice. A digital version is available at Boom™ Learning for an additional fee.

Word	Sentence
1. blossom	Did the tree blossom?
2. common	That is not a common cat.
3. locket	Did he drop the locket?
4. oblong	He went past the oblong box.
5. pocket	He stuck it in his pocket.
6. jumble	It is in a jumble.
7. muffin	Is the muffin sweet?
8. nutmeg	Is that nutmeg on top of it?
9. puzzle	Can he solve the puzzle?
10. sudden	He felt a sudden need to run.

/10

DICTATION

Open Syllable WORDS

based on *The Raven Remix*
by Carolee Dean

Directions: The following sentences may be used for dictation, spelling, articulation, and/or reading practice. A digital version is available at Boom™ Learning for an additional fee.

Word	Sentence
raven	Can a raven sing?
table	He sat at the table.
sequin	Did the vest have a sequin on it?
relax	He cannot relax.
final	It was the final math test.
silent	The kitchen is silent.
bonus	He got a bonus tip.
robot	Is the bug a robot?
gluten	Did the muffin have gluten in it?
Pluto	Pluto is a cat.

/10

DICTATION

S WORDS

based on *The Raven Remix*
by Carolee Dean

Directions: The following sentences may be used for dictation, spelling, articulation, and/or reading practice. A digital version is available at Boom™ Learning for an additional fee.

Word	Sentence
sudden	I felt a sudden gust of wind.
silent	It was silent in the kitchen.
simple	It was a simple wooden chest.
socket	The bug had black sockets.
solve	Did he solve the riddle?
skillet	He will cook it in a skillet.
splendid	It is a splendid chest.
sleeping	Is the cat sleeping?
snacked	He snacked on shrimp.
spiral	Is that a spiral ham?

/10

DICTATION

R WORDS

based on *The Raven Remix*
by Carolee Dean

Directions: The following sentences may be used for dictation, spelling, articulation, and/or reading practice. A digital version is available at Boom™ Learning for an additional fee.

Word	Sentence
reddish	Did it have reddish skin?
request	Did he request a snack?
resting	It is resting on the shelf.
riddle	Did he solve the riddle?
relax	Can he relax?
broken	The leg of the bug is broken.
creeping	Is it creeping next to him?
drifted	He drifted in.
greeted	The man greeted him.
sprinted	He sprinted from the kitchen.

/10

DICTATION

L WORDS

based on *The Raven Remix*
by Carolee Dean

Directions: The following sentences may be used for dictation, spelling, articulation, and/or reading practice. A digital version is available at Boom™ Learning for an additional fee.

Word	Sentence
ladle	He had a ladle in his hand.
little	Ed set up a little picnic.
middle	A vest was in the middle of the chest.
pickle	He had a pickle for a snack.
puzzle	The puzzle is in a nook.
riddle	Is it a book of riddles?
kettle	Is the kettle top ringing?
simple	It was a simple wooden chest.
table	Is it on the table?
maple	Is that maple in the bacon?

/10

ALPHABET CODE BREAKERS

based on *The Raven Remix*
by Carolee Dean

INTRODUCTION

Poe used a cryptograph, a message written in code, in his story "The Gold Bug." The characters in the story had to figure out the key to the code and decipher a secret message to find a treasure left on an island by Captain Kidd, a famous pirate.

In Code Breakers #1, figure out the pattern for the key code to decipher short phrases about cats.

In Code Breakers #2, use the same key code to decipher longer idioms about cats.

To discover the meaning of the phrases and idioms, see **The Cat's Meow** activity in the VOCABULARY AND SEMANTICS section. It includes Catty Idioms and Feline Phrases.

The Raven Remix also contains a cryptograph. Some parts of the key for that cryptograph are provided in Code Breakers #3. Figure out the pattern, then decipher the message.

PRACTICE MAKES PERFECT
Start by using the ABC cards on the next page to practice quickly saying the missing letter. This will help you solve the puzzles on the next few pages. First, practice the cards in order. Then, mix them up. These cards are also available on Boom™ Learning for a small additional fee.

ALPHABET ORDER

Also available online as Boom™ Cards
from *The Raven Remix*
by Carolee Dean

A B C _

B C D _

C D E _

D E F _

E F G _

F G H _

G H I _

H I J _

I J K _

J K L _

K L M _

L M N _

M N O _

N O P _

ALPHABET ORDER
continued
from *The Raven Remix*
by Carolee Dean

O P Q _

P Q R _

Q R S _

R S T _

S T U _

T U V _

U V W _

V W X _

W X Y _

ALPHABET CODE BREAKERS #1

based on *The Raven Remix*
by Carolee Dean

Directions:
1. Use the example to figure out the pattern in the key below.
2. Fill in the rest of the key and decipher the secret Feline Phrases.
3. Check your answers on the next page.

Cat Idioms & Phrases

Example: **ezs   bzs**

              <u>**fat**</u>   <u>**cat**</u>

1. r b z q d c x   b z s

   _ _ _ _ _ _ _   _ _ _

2. b z s m z o

   _ _ _ _ _ _

3. b z s   a t q f k z q

   _ _ _   _ _ _ _ _ _ _

4. b n o x b z s

   _ _ _ _ _ _ _

5. b z s ' r   l d n v

   _ _ _ ' _   _ _ _ _

Key

a = b	n =
b = c	o =
c =	p =
d =	q =
e = f	r =
f =	s = t
g =	t =
h =	u =
i =	v =
j =	w =
k =	x =
l =	y =
m =	z = a

ALPHABET CODE BREAKERS #1

based on *The Raven Remix*
by Carolee Dean

ANSWERS

Cat Phrases
Example: ezs   bzs
fat cat
1. rbzqdcx bzs
scaredy cat
2. bzsmzo
catnap
3. bzs atqfkzq
cat burglar
4. bnoxbzs
copycat
5. bzs'r ldnv
cat's meow

Key

a = b	n = o
b = c	o = p
c = d	p = q
d = e	q = r
e = f	r = s
f = g	s = t
g = h	t = u
h = i	u = v
i = j	v = w
j = k	w = x
k = l	x = y
l = m	y = z
m = n	z = a

ALPHABET CODE BREAKERS #2

based on *The Raven Remix*
by Carolee Dean

Now that you are an expert code breaker, use the key code from the last activity to decipher the Catty Idioms below.

Catty Idioms

1. Cnm's kds sgd bzs nts ne sgd azf.

   _ _ _ ' _   _ _ _   _ _ _   _ _ _   _ _ _   _ _   _ _ _   _ _ _.

2. Hs'r qzhmhmf bzsr zmc cnfr.

   _ _ ' _   _ _ _ _ _ _ _   _ _ _ _   _ _ _   _ _ _ _.

3. Knnj vgzs sgd bzs cqzffdc hm.

   _ _ _ _   _ _ _ _   _ _ _   _ _ _   _ _ _ _ _ _ _   _ _.

4. Btqhnrhsx jhkkdc sgd bzs.

   _ _ _ _ _ _ _ _ _   _ _ _ _ _ _   _ _ _   _ _ _

5. Hs'r khjd gdqchmf bzsr.

   _ _ ' _   _ _ _ _   _ _ _ _ _ _ _   _ _ _ _.

ALPHABET CODE BREAKERS #2

based on *The Raven Remix*
by Carolee Dean

ANSWERS

Catty Idioms

1. Cnm's kds sgd bzs nts ne sgd azf.

   Don't let the cat out of the bag.

2. Hs'r qzhmhmf bzsr zmc cnfr

   It's raining cats and dogs.

3. Knnj vgzs sgd bzs cqzffdc hm

   Look what the cat dragged in.

4. Btqhnrhsx jhkkdc sgd bzs

   Curiosity killed the cat.

5. Hs'r khjd gdqchmf bzsr.

   It's like herding cats.

ALPHABET CODE BREAKERS #3

Complete the Key
based on *The Raven Remix*
by Carolee Dean

Poe used a cryptograph, a message written in code, in his story "The Gold Bug." The characters in the story had to figure out the key to the code and decipher a secret message to find a treasure. *The Raven Remix* also contains a cryptograph. Some parts of the key for that cryptograph are below. Figure out the pattern, then fill in the rest of the key. Finally, check your answers on the next page and then use the key to decipher the secret message.

*A is B and B is C
C is D and D is E
Z is A and O is P
And at the end, S equals T*

Bzo'm Jhcc nmbd rodms z vddj

Vhsghm sgd hmm zr gd chc rddj

Z rons sn rszrg ghr qnbjr zmc bzrg,

Z ghccdm rons, Z rons sn jddo

Z rhlokd zlokd vnncdm bgdrs.

Fn knnj enq hs zs ghr qdptdrs.

Key

a = b	n =
b = c	o = p
c = d	p =
d = e	q =
e =	r =
f =	s = t
g =	t =
h =	u =
i =	v =
j =	w =
k =	x =
l =	y =
m =	z = a

ALPHABET CODE BREAKERS #3

ANSWERS

based on *The Raven Remix*
by Carolee Dean

Use the key below to figure out the secret message on the next page.

Key

a = b	n = o
b = c	o = p
c = d	p = q
d = e	q = r
e = f	r = s
f = g	s = t
g = h	t = u
h = i	u = v
i = j	v = w
j = k	w = x
k = l	x = y
l = m	y = z
m = n	z = a

ALPHABET CODE BREAKERS #3

Solve the Cryptograph

based on *The Raven Remix*

by Carolee Dean

Use the key code on the previous page to figure out the secret message below from the book.

Bzo'm Jhcc nmbd rodms z vddj

_____

Vhsghm sgd hmm zr gd chc rddj

_____

Z rons sn rszrg ghr qnbjr zmc bzrg,

_____

Z ghccdm rons, Z rons sn jddo

_____

Z rhlokd zlokd vnncdm bgdrs.

_____

Fn knnj enq hs zs ghr qdptdrs.

_____

ALPHABET CODE BREAKERS #3
Solve the Cryptograph

ANSWER

Cap'n Kidd once spent a week

Within the inn as he did seek

a spot to stash his rocks and cash,

A hidden spot, a spot to keep

A simple, ample wooden chest.

Go look for it at his request.

In *The Raven Remix*, a young man and a strange innkeeper use the code on the previous page to find a treasure chest. Go to the **Secret Codes** activity in the CREATE section to learn how to create a code of your own.

PHONOLOGICAL AWARENESS

INTRODUCTION

Phonological Awareness is one of the foundational Components of Reading (COR). Learn more about this important skill on the COR INSTRUCTION page at https://wordtravelpress.com/.

Phonological awareness includes rhyming, counting syllables, and detecting initial, final, and medial sounds or phonemes. Prosody has also been included which involves recognizing the suprasegmental features of words such as rhythm, stress, pitch, and intonation.

Phonemic awareness is the part of phonological awareness that deals specifically with individual sounds. Students work with syllables and phonemes in the following activities by isolating, segmenting, adding, deleting, and substituting.

Phonemic skills are first taught as an oral skill (without letters) in the oral exercises found in the **Say It Again, Sam** activity. But phonemic awareness has the greatest impact when sounds are paired with letters and integrated with writing and spelling (Paulson, 2018 p. 234). In the **Sound Tracks** activity, students change one sound at a time to create new words. In **Rhyme Time** they work with the concepts of rhyme and alliteration with the added component of writing a sentence containing an alliteration. In **Feel the Beat**, students identify the stressed syllables in a line of poetry. In the **Dictation** activity in the previous section, students draw upon their knowledge of sound-letter correspondences to write short sentences to dictation. The sentences in **Dictation** may also be used for reading practice.

Activities are described in more detail below:

Say It Again, Sam—Students work on deletion by repeating words and leaving out sounds or syllables. They start by deleting the first syllable from a two-syllable word. Next, they delete the second syllable. Then, they delete the initial sounds, final sounds, and medial sounds. The medial sounds are parts of consonant blends. They are more difficult to isolate than single consonants. In this way, students move from more basic to more challenging phonological and phoneme awareness activities.

For a deeper and much more extensive exploration of phoneme awareness, see *Equipped for Reading Success: A Comprehensive, Step-By-Step Program for Developing Phonemic Awareness and Fluent Word Recognition* by David Kilpatrick.

See the following page for additional phonological awareness activities.

Continued

Feel the Beat, students underline the stressed words in lines of a poem. Then they read the poem by exaggerating the underlined words. They do this by saying the stressed syllables longer, louder, and with a slightly higher pitch. Next, they incorporate two-syllable words and draw drumsticks above the stressed syllable. Finally, they read the poems with normal stress. Ask them if they can still feel the beat. If not, instruct them to try reading the poem like a robot, giving every word the same stress. Then read the poem again with stress on the highlighted syllables to bring out the difference.

In **Rhyme Time #1**, students circle words that rhyme and underline alliterations (words that start with the same sound). They then create a sentence that uses alliteration. This process also helps them understand and use literary devices. Additionally, switching between these three tasks requires students to use cognitive flexibility at both the letter-sound and meaning levels. Some students may not be ready to switch between tasks. For them, do one task at a time. For a metacognitive activity, ask students to think about how they tackle tasks. Would they rather complete all three steps for each target word before moving on OR would they prefer to do all the rhymes first, then all the alliterations, and then all the sentences? Get them talking about their internal processes and preferences.

Advanced students may be interested in a discussion of rhythm and meter. In **Rhyme Time #2 and #3**, students analyze the rhyme scheme of "The Raven." In **Rhyme Time #4**, they create their own Poem Parody.

References:

Kilpatrick, D.A. (2016). Equipped for reading success: A comprehensive, step-by-step program for developing phonemic awareness and fluent word recognition. Syracuse, NY: Casey & Kirsch Publishers.

Paulson, L. H. (2018). Teaching phonemic awareness. In J.R. Birsh & S. Carreker (Eds.) *Multisensory teaching of basic language skills* (4th ed., pp. 205-253). Baltimore, MD: Paul H. Brookes Publishing Co.

Say It Again, Sam
Two-Syllable Words

Initial Syllable Deletion
based on *The Raven Remix*
by Carolee Dean

Directions:
The teacher says a two-syllable word. The student repeats the word. The teacher says which syllable to delete. The student says the syllable that is left. Note that the stress is on the second syllable.

Teacher	student	Teacher	Student
Say….		Say it again but leave out…	
intent	**intent**	/in/	**tent**
within	**within**	/with/	**in**
banshee	**banshee**	/ban/	**she**
relax	**relax**	/re/	**lax**
request	**request**	/re/	**quest**
dismiss	**dismiss**	/dis/	**miss**
insist	**insist**	/in/	**sist**
upset	**upset**	/up/	**set**
compel	**compel**	/cum/	**pel**
regret	**regret**	/re/	**gret**

/10

Say It Again, Sam
Two-Syllable Words

Final Syllable Deletion
based on *The Raven Remix*
by Carolee Dean

Directions:
The teacher says a two-syllable word. The student repeats the word. The teacher says which syllable to delete. The student says the syllable that is left. Note that the stress in the initial word is on the first syllable.

Teacher	student	Teacher	Student
Say....		Say it again but leave out...	
bolo	**bolo**	/lo/	**bo**
maple	**maple**	/pl/	**may**
locust	**locust**	/kust/	**low**
student	**student**	/dent/	**stu**
sequin	**sequin**	/kwin/	**see**
fabric	**fabric**	/rik/	**fab**
nutmeg	**nutmeg**	/meg/	**nut**
skillet	**skillet**	/let/	**skill**
insect	**insect**	/sect/	**in**
plumcot	**plumcot**	/kot/	**plum**

/10

Say It Again, Sam
One-Syllable Words

Initial /s/ Sound Deletion in Blends
based on *The Raven Remix*
by Carolee Dean

Directions: The teacher says the word. The student repeats the word. The teacher says which sound to delete. The student says what is left. Tell the student that some (but not all) will result in real words.

Teacher	student	Teacher	Student
Say....		Say it again but leave out...	
skipping	**skipping**	/s/	**kipping**
spiral	**spiral**	/s/	**piral**
sleeping	**sleeping**	/s/	**leeping**
scramble	**scramble**	/s/	**cramble**
stacking	**stacking**	/s/	**tacking**
stopping	**stopping**	/s/	**topping**
strudel	**strudel**	/s/	**trudel**
skillet	**skillet**	/s/	**killet**
swinging	**swinging**	/s/	**winging**
stinging	**stinging**	/s/	**tinging**

/10

Say It Again, Sam
One-Syllable Words

R Blend - Initial Sound Deletion in Blends
based on *The Raven Remix*
by Carolee Dean

Directions: The teacher says the word. The student repeats the word. The teacher says which sound to delete. The student says what is left. Tell the student that some (but not all) will result in real words.

Teacher	student	Teacher	Student
Say….		Say it again but leave out…	
broken	**broken**	/b/	**roken**
crashing	**crashing**	/k/	**rashing**
creeping	**creeping**	/k/	**reeping**
crested	**crested**	/k/	**rested**
drifted	**drifted**	/d/	**rifted**
greeted	**greeted**	/g/	**reeted**
printed	**printed**	/p/	**rinted**
screeched	**screeched**	/s/	**creeched**
pricking	**pricking**	/p/	**ricking**
sprinted	**sprinted**	/s/	**printed**

/10

Say It Again, Sam
One-Syllable Words

Final Sound Deletion - /l/

based on *The Raven Remix*
by Carolee Dean

Directions: The teacher says the word. The student repeats the word. The teacher says which sound to delete. The student says what is left. Some may be non-words.

Teacher	student	Teacher	Student
Say….		Say it again but leave out…	
riddle	riddle	/l/	rid
ladle	ladle	/l/	laid
simple	simple	/l/	simp
apple	apple	/l/	app
middle	middle	/l/	mid
pickle	pickle	/l/	pick
needle	needle	/l/	need
maple	maple	/l/	mape
puzzle	puzzle	/l/	puzz
table	table	/l/	tabe

/10

101

Say It Again, Sam
One-Syllable Words

Medial /r/ Sound Deletion
based on *The Raven Remix*
by Carolee Dean

Directions: The teacher says the word. The student repeats the word. The teacher says which sound to delete. The student says what is left. Some may be non-words

Teacher	student	Teacher	Student
Say....		Say it again but leave out...	
broken	**broken**	/r/	**boken**
crashing	**crashing**	/r/	**cashing**
creeping	**creeping**	/r/	**keeping**
grabbing	**grabbing**	/r/	**gabbing**
pricking	**pricking**	/r/	**picking**
drifted	**drifted**	/r/	**difted**
grunted	**grunted**	/r/	**gunted**
crested	**crested**	/r/	**kested**
tricking	**tricking**	/r/	**ticking**
trashing	**trashing**	/r/	**tashing**

/10

SOUND TRACKS
based on *The Raven Remix*
by Carolee Dean

Directions: The teacher says the first word. The student repeats the word and uses the Sound Tracks Letters at the end of this section to construct the word saying each sound. The student then reads the entire word. The teacher then says another word with one sound changed. The student says the new word, makes the sound change saying each sound, then reads the entire word. Some of the words may be non-words. Letters are also available for FREE on Boom Cards. For lists 2 and 3, the student needs to be familiar with the idea that **/k/** is spelled with a **c** when it comes before a consonant.

List 1 – Initial /s/ blends	List 2 – Initial /r/ blends	List 3 – Initial /l/ Blends	List 4 - final blends
slip	hint	lap	amp
stip	rint	flap	tamp
strip	print	flip	stamp
strap	sprint	lip	stap
trap	sprunt	lid	stad
tap	prunt	lim	stand
stap	runt	lam	sand
stop	rust	slam	land
top	rest	slim	lad
pot	crest	slip	lat
spot	crust	slap	last
sot	crost	lap	fast
slot	rost	clap	fant
lot	rot	clip	pant
lit	rat	clop	plant

/45

SOUND TRACKS
Letters

Directions: Cut out the letters below to use for the Sound Tracks Activity. Enlarge as needed from the downloadable resources and glue onto card stock to make them easier to pick up. A digital version of the activity may be found for FREE at Boom™ Learning at

https://wow.boomlearning.com. Explore Store>Word Travel Press.

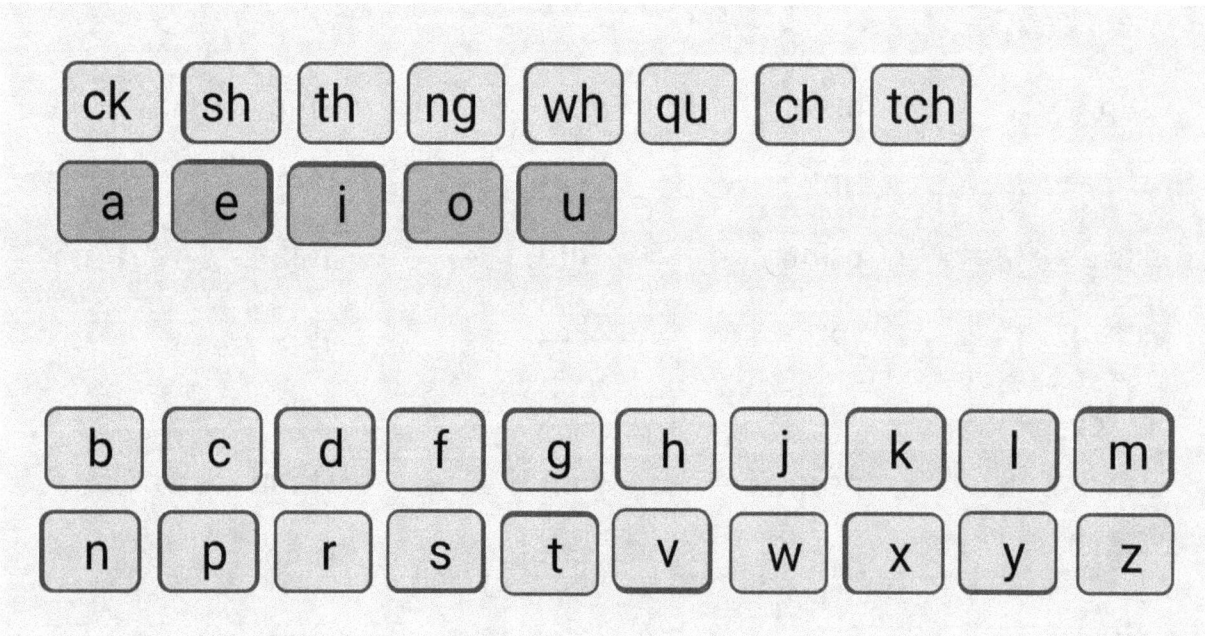

Feel the Beat #1
based on *The Raven Remix*
by Carolee Dean

Directions: Read the lines of poetry below.

1. Underline each stressed beat following the pattern shown in the first two lines. The first stressed beat in each line has been done for you.
2. Read this section of the story out loud and exaggerate the stressed words.
3. Read the lines of poetry again, but this time in your normal voice.
4. Can you still feel the beat?

Excerpt from *The Raven Remix* (from Level 3 of the The HOT ROD series)

<u>Once</u> up<u>on</u> a <u>week</u> of <u>test</u>ing,
<u>sick</u> of <u>sums</u>, I <u>need</u>ed <u>rest</u>ing,
<u>so</u>, I left my final class
and <u>went</u> into the Ed. A. P.
<u>Book</u> Stop, Pet Shop, Inn and Grill
to <u>get</u> a snack, relax, and chill.
<u>Stand</u>ing on a wooden sill,
a <u>stun</u>ning raven looked at me.
<u>From</u> the jacket of a book,
the <u>cun</u>ning raven peered at me.
"<u>Have</u> a peek within," said she.

ANSWERS

Excerpt from *The Raven Remix* (from Level 3 of the The HOT ROD series)

<u>Once</u> up<u>on</u> a <u>week</u> of <u>te</u>sting,
<u>sick</u> of <u>sums</u>, I <u>nee</u>ded <u>res</u>ting,
<u>so</u>, I <u>left</u> my <u>fi</u>nal <u>class</u>
and <u>went</u> in<u>to</u> the <u>Ed</u>. A. <u>P.</u>
<u>Book</u> Stop, <u>Pet</u> Shop, <u>Inn</u> and <u>Grill</u>
to <u>get</u> a <u>snack</u>, rel<u>ax</u>, and <u>chill</u>.
<u>Stan</u>ding <u>on</u> a <u>woo</u>den <u>sill,</u>
a <u>stun</u>ning <u>ra</u>ven <u>looked</u> at <u>me</u>.
<u>From</u> the <u>ja</u>cket <u>of</u> a <u>book</u>,
the <u>cun</u>ning <u>ra</u>ven <u>peered</u> at me.
"<u>Have</u> a peek wit<u>hin</u>," said <u>she</u>.

Feel the Beat #2

based on *The Raven Remix*
by Carolee Dean

Directions: Read the lines of poetry below.
1. Draw a drumstick above each stressed beat. Follow the pattern in the first few lines.
2. Read the poem and tap the stressed syllables with a pencil or drumstick.
3. Read the lines of poetry again, but this time in your normal voice.
4. Can you still feel the beat?

Excerpt from *The Raven Remix* (Level 3 – The HOT ROD series)

/   /   /   /

Sitting, I began to settle.

/   /   /   /

Ed filled up a little kettle,

/   /   /   /

chopped up chicken, pitted plumcots,

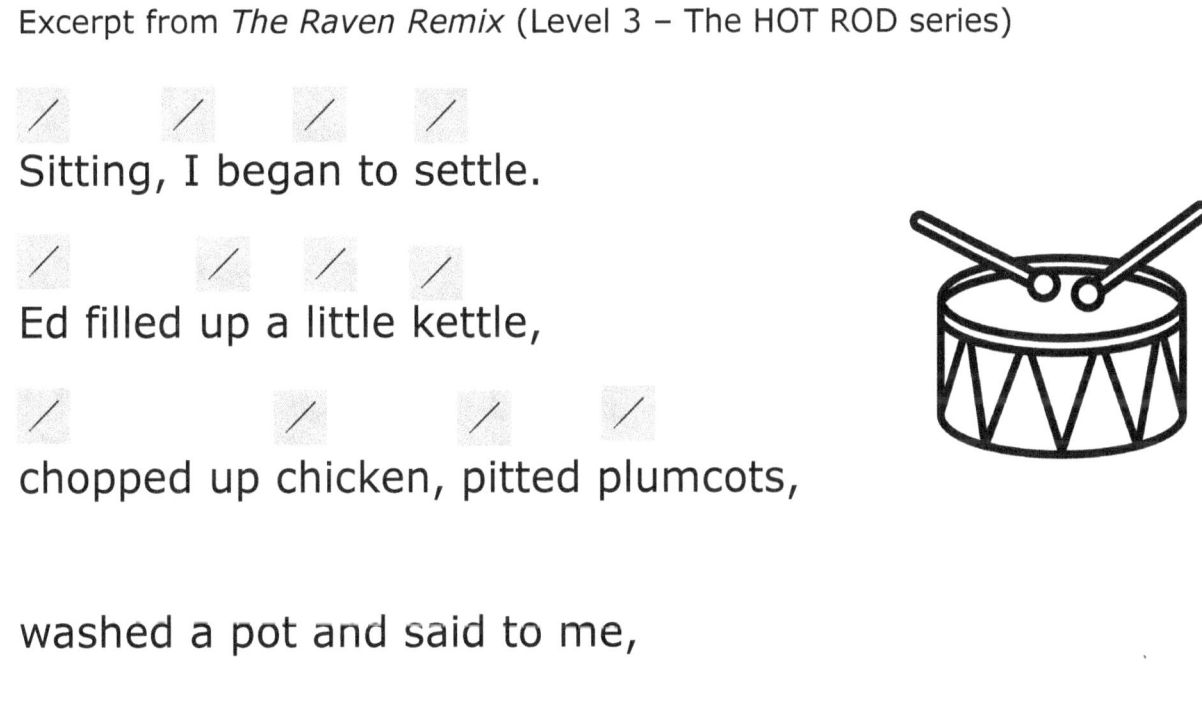

washed a pot and said to me,

"Skipping math class is not prudent,

but we relish helping students.

Just watch out for kitten mutants.

We have pets you have not seen."

ANSWERS

Sitting, I began to settle.

Ed filled up a little kettle,

chopped up chicken, pitted plumcots,

washed a pot and said to me,

"Skipping math class is not prudent,

but we relish helping students.

Just watch out for kitten mutants.

We have pets you have not seen."

Rhyme Time #1
based on *The Raven Remix*
by Carolee Dean

Directions: Read the target words below, and then:
1. Circle words that rhyme with it.
2. Underline words that start with the same consonant blend. This is called *alliteration.*
3. Use the target word and a word that starts with the same consonant blends to write a sentence. Use another piece of paper if needed.

1. grinning   (spinning)   <u>greenish</u>   blossom   <u>grabbing</u>

Sentence: The grinning man was grabbing rings.

2. broken   bridle   token   scramble   brittle

Sentence:

3. student   printed   stinging   prudent   standing

Sentence:

4. spiral   reddish   splendid   speckle   viral   spelling

Sentence:

5. crashing   creeping   flashing   strudel   smashing

Sentence:

6. flinging   singing   flapping   stinging   flopping

Sentence:

7. sleeping   slumping   creeping   slinging   greeting

Sentence:

8. skillet   millet   broken   skipping   skidding

Sentence:

Rhyme Time #1
based on *The Raven Remix*
by Carolee Dean

ANSWERS

1. grinning   spinning   greenish   blossom   grabbing

Sentence: The grinning man was grabbing rings.

2. broken   bridle   token   scramble   brittle

Sentence:

3. student   printed   stinging   prudent   standing

Sentence:

4. spiral   reddish   pricking   speckle   viral   spelling

Sentence:

5. crashing   creeping   flashing   strudel   smashing

Sentence:

6. flinging   singing   flapping   stinging   flopping

Sentence:

7. sleeping   slumping   creeping   slinging   greeting

Sentence:

8. skillet   millet   broken   skipping   skidding

Sentence:

Rhyme Time #2
Analyzing Meter
based on *The Raven Remix*
by Carolee Dean

The Raven Remix follows the rhyme scheme of "The Raven." The first stanza of the poem is below for reference.

Underline the stressed beats. The first two lines are done for you.

<u>On</u>ce upon a <u>mid</u>night <u>drea</u>ry, <u>while</u> I <u>pon</u>dered, <u>weak</u> and <u>wea</u>ry,
<u>O</u>ver <u>ma</u>ny a <u>quaint</u> and <u>cu</u>rious <u>vol</u>ume <u>of</u> for<u>got</u>ten <u>lore</u>—
     While I nodded, nearly napping, suddenly there came a tapping,
As of someone gently rapping, rapping at my chamber door.
"'Tis some visitor," I muttered, "tapping at my chamber door—.
     Only this and nothing more."

A pattern of stressed and unstressed syllables is called a "foot."
How many beats or feet are in each line (for lines 1-5)?_____

The length of the meter is described by using Greek terms, such as:
Monometer: One foot
Dimeter: Two feet
Trimeter: Three feet
Tetrameter: Four feet
Pentameter: Five feet
Hexameter: Six feet
Heptameter: Seven feet
Octameter: Eight feet

Which meter is used in The Raven: _____

If the stress is on the first syllable of a two-syllable "foot," that pattern is called an iamb or iambic: Da-DUM, da-DUM, da-DUM, da-DUM

If the stress is on the second syllable of a two-syllable "foot," that pattern is called a trochee or trochaic: DA-dum, DA-dum, DA-dum, DA-dum

Which stress pattern is used in "The Raven?" _____

Which term best describes "The Raven? Circle your answer.
A. Iambic Tetrameter
B. Trochaic Dimeter
C. Trochaic Octameter
D. Iambic Octameter

ANSWERS

Underline the stressed beats. The first two lines are done for you.

Once up<u>on</u> a <u>mid</u>night <u>drea</u>ry, <u>while</u> I <u>pon</u>dered, <u>weak</u> and <u>wea</u>ry,
<u>O</u>ver <u>ma</u>ny a <u>quaint</u> and <u>cur</u>ious <u>vol</u>ume <u>of</u> forgotten <u>lore</u>—
    While I <u>nod</u>ded, <u>near</u>ly <u>nap</u>ping, <u>sud</u>denly there <u>came</u> a <u>tap</u>ping,
<u>As</u> of <u>some</u>one <u>gent</u>ly <u>rap</u>ping, <u>rap</u>ping <u>at</u> my <u>cham</u>ber <u>door</u>.
"'<u>Tis</u> some <u>vis</u>i<u>tor</u>," I <u>mut</u>tered, "<u>tap</u>ping <u>at</u> my <u>cham</u>ber <u>door</u>—.
    <u>On</u>ly <u>this</u> and <u>no</u>thing <u>more</u>."

How many beats or feet are in each line (for lines 1-5)? <u>8</u>

Which meter is used in The Raven: <u>Octameter</u>

Which stress pattern is used in "The Raven?" <u>Trochee or Trochaic</u>

Which term best describes "The Raven? Circle your answer.
C. Trochaic Octameter

Rhyme Time #3
Analyzing Rhyme Scheme
"The Raven"
based on *The Raven Remix*
by Carolee Dean

You can figure out the rhyme scheme or pattern of a poem by labeling the last word of each line of verse with a letter of the alphabet, starting with A. Each final word that rhymes with a previous word is assigned that same letter. See the example below.

Once upon a midnight dreary, while I pondered, weak and **weary**,	A
Over many a quaint and curious volume of forgotten **lore**—	B
While I nodded, nearly napping, suddenly there came a **tapping**,	C
As of someone gently rapping, rapping at my chamber **door**.	B
"'Tis some visitor," I muttered, "tapping at my chamber **door**—.	B
Only this and nothing **more**."	B

Practice this concept by analyzing the rhyme scheme of the poem below:

Jack Sprat

Jack Sprat could eat no fat,

His wife could eat no lean.

And so between them both, you see,

They licked the platter clean.

Rhyme Time #3
Analyzing Rhyme Scheme
"The Raven"
based on *The Raven Remix*
by Carolee Dean

Although the basic rhyme scheme of "The Raven" is ABCBBB, there are also many internal rhymes. An internal rhyme is one that happens when two or more words in one line rhyme. In order to create a parody of "The Raven," it was necessary to breakdown the rhyme pattern even further. An X was used for line 3 and 9 because in some verses of "The Raven," these lines do rhyme.

Once upon a midnight dreary,	A
while I pondered, weak and weary,	A
Over many a quaint and curious	X
volume of forgotten lore—.	B
While I nodded, nearly napping,	C
suddenly there came a tapping,	C
As of someone gently rapping,	C
rapping at my chamber door—.	B
"'Tis some visitor," I muttered,	X
"Tapping at my chamber door—.	B
Only this and nothing more."	B

Observe how this pattern was followed in the *The Raven Remix*. If you have the book, circle the rhyming words in the poem. Put an X on final words that do not rhyme. The first one is done for you.

1	dreary	A	testing	Once upon a week of (testing,)
2	weary	A	resting	sick of sums, I needed resting,
3	curious	X	class	so, I skipped my final class
4	lore	B	P.	and went into the Ed A. P.
5	napping	C	grill	Book Stop, Pet Shop, Inn and Grill
6	tapping	C	chill	to get a snack, relax, and chill.
7	rapping	C	sill	Standing on a wooden sill,
8	door	B	me	a stunning raven looked at me.
9	muttered	X	book	From the jacket of a book,
10	door	B (repeat)	me	The cunning raven peered at me.
11	more	B	she	"Have a peek within," said she.

Rhyme Time #3
Analyzing Rhyme Scheme
"The Raven"

based on *The Raven Remix*
by Carolee Dean

ANSWERS

1	dreary	A	testing	Once upon a week of testing
2	weary	A	resting	sick of sums, I needed resting,
3	curious	X	class	so, I skipped my final class
4	lore	B	P.	and went into the Ed A. P.
5	napping	C	grill	Book Stop, Pet Shop, Inn and Grill
6	tapping	C	chill	to get a snack, relax, and chill.
7	rapping	C	sill	Standing on a wooden sill,
8	door	B	me	a stunning raven looked at me.
9	muttered	X	book	From the jacket of a book,
10	door	B (repeat)	me	The cunning raven peered at me.
11	more	B	she	"Have a peek within," said she.

©2025 Word Travel Press LLC - www.wordtravelpress.com

Rhyme Time #4
Create a Poem Parody
based on *The Raven Remix*
by Carolee Dean

Study the pattern for The Raven Remix below. Then create your own poem parody.

1	dreary	A	testing	Once upon a week of testing,
2	weary	A	resting	sick of sums, I needed resting,
3	curious	X	class	so, I skipped my final class
4	lore	B	P.	and went into the Ed A. P.
5	napping	C	grill	Book Stop, Pet Shop, Inn and Grill
6	tapping	C	chill	to get a snack, relax, and chill.
7	rapping	C	sill	Standing on a wooden sill,
8	door	B	me	a stunning raven looked at me.
9	muttered	X	book	From the jacket of a book,
10	door	B (repeat)	me	The cunning raven peered at me.
11	more	B	she	"Have a peek within," said she.

Create your own parody below. See how far you can get. Use a separate piece of paper if needed. **If you prefer, use "Jack Sprat" from Rhyme Time #3.**

1	dreary	A	
2	weary	A	
3	curious	X	
4	lore	B	
5	napping	C	
6	tapping	C	
7	rapping	C	
8	door	B	
9	muttered	X	
10	door	B	
11	more	B	

Cognitive Flexibility

INTRODUCTION

What is Cognitive Flexibility

Cognitive flexibility is an important executive function skill that centers on the ability to switch between different types of information. It can involve switching between different tasks or thinking about more than one concept at a time. Working memory is an important element of cognitive flexibility that helps a person manage more than one task, concept, or piece of information at the same time. It impacts reading, writing, spelling, and more.

How Cognitive Flexibility Impacts Reading

Specific to reading, cognitive flexibility is essential for both decoding and comprehension. Students need cognitive flexibility to be able to hold different possible pronunciations for a letter or combination of letters in mind while decoding unfamiliar words. At the same time, they must consider the word's meaning. Working memory enables a reader to compare the possible pronunciations of a word with words in their lexicon (internal dictionary). While they are figuring out how to pronounce the word and determining what the word means, a reader must also hold the rest of the sentence in mind. The content and structure of the sentence will also affect the meaning of the word. If a word has multiple meanings, cognitive flexibility is required to hold the possible options in short-term memory while making judgments about the best fit within the context of the sentence and paragraph.

While many tasks are useful for developing cognitive flexibility, not many directly relate to reading and decoding. The activities on the next few pages were designed to address executive function skills that directly relate to a structured literacy scope and sequence. By sorting words that belong to two different categories simultaneously, students can work on cognitive flexibility.

Cognitive Flexibility

For more information about Cognitive Flexibility as well as a FREE printable activity based on Level 1 of the HOT ROD series (CVC, CCVC, CVCC, CCCVC, etc), visit the Cognitive Flexibility Page at www.wordtravelpress.com.

The *Cognitive Flexibility Category Sorts & Multiple Classification Tasks for Closed Syllables* is a 38- page PDF filled with lists containing closed syllable words that can be cut out and sorted according to a variety of categories.

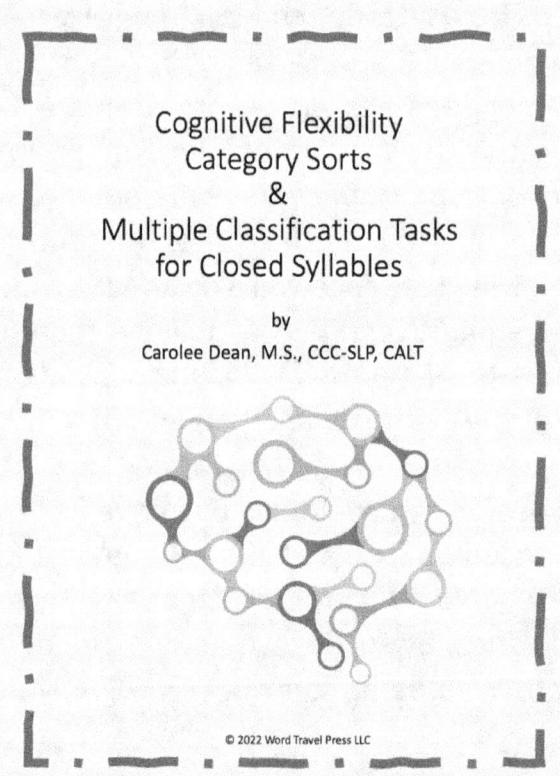

Cognitive Flexibility
Category Sorts
&
Multiple Classification Tasks
for Closed Syllables

by
Carolee Dean, M.S., CCC-SLP, CALT

© 2022 Word Travel Press LLC

Cognitive Flexibility Online Game

In addition to the printable resource on the previous page, A FREE Digital Boom Card activity is available online. See the Downloadable Resources page near the end of the book for details or go to https://wow.boomlearning.com and explore Store>Word Travel Press. Additional digital resources are available on that page. Some are free and some have an additional charge.

The target words in the free online Boom game are from Category Sort #1 – Food and Objects.

This digital Boom Deck has three component parts:
1. First, students sort words into two categories: (ex. Foods vs. Objects). You may read any unfamiliar words to students.
2. Next, they sort the SAME cards into two different categories: Open vs. Closed Syllables (found in the first syllable of a word).
    (Note: reproducible activities for these category sorts may be found on the following pages.)
3. Finally, students sort the same words on a 2x2 matrix in the Multiple Classification Activity while considering all 4 categories at once. This step should be completed directly after steps 1 and 2 for each individual sort. The template for this activity is on page 139. See tips for scaffolding responses for the Multiple Classification Activity on pages 137-138.

The lists for this sorting activity are taken directly from a Cognitive Flexibility study conducted by Carolee Dean and Kelly Cartwright, Ph.D. For additional information, contact info@wordtravelpress.com.

References:
Cartwright, K.B. (2023). _Executive skills and reading comprehension: A guide for educators_ (Second Edition). New York, NY: Guildford Press.

Tunmer, W.E., & Chapman, J.W. (2012). Does set for variability mediate the influence of vocabulary knowledge on the development of word recognition skills? _Scientific Studies of Reading_, 16(2), 122-140.

Vadasy, P.F., Sanders, E.A., Cartwright, K.B. (2022). Cognitive flexibility in beginning decoding and encoding. _The Journal of Education for Students Placed at Risk_, in press.

Zipke, M. (2016). The importance of flexibility of pronunciation in learning to decode: A training study in set for variability. _First Language_. 36 (1), 71-86.

Cognitive Flexibility
Category Sort
Open vs. Closed Syllables
(found in the first syllable of the word)

Directions:
1. Use the words found in the eight lists that follow.
2. After sorting a list into semantic categories, sort the same words by syllable type using the chart below.

Open   # Closed

Cognitive Flexibility
Category Sort #1
Foods vs. Objects

Directions: Cut out the words and set them in the correct category.

robot	saddle	pickle	apple
muffin	puzzle	cradle	bacon
strudel	sequin	basil	candle

Foods   Objects

Cognitive Flexibility
Category Sort #1
Foods vs. Objects

ANSWERS

Foods

muffin	basil
strudel	bacon
pickle	apple

Objects

cradle	puzzle
sequin	candle
robot	saddle

Open

strudel	cradle
basil	sequin
bacon	robot

Closed

muffin	puzzle
pickle	candle
apple	saddle

Cognitive Flexibility
Category Sort #2
Kitchen Items vs. Actions

Directions: Cut out the words and set them in the correct category.

table	kettle	wiggle	juggle
gobble	skillet	ladle	open
stifle	utensil	focus	griddle

Kitchen Items   Actions

Cognitive Flexibility
Category Sort #2
Kitchen Items vs. Actions

ANSWERS

Kitchen Items

ladle	griddle
skillet	utensil
table	kettle

Actions

gobble	open
focus	stifle
wiggle	juggle

Open

ladle	focus
table	open
utensil	stifle

Closed

skillet	gobble
griddle	wiggle
kettle	juggle

Cognitive Flexibility
Category Sort #3
Animals vs. People

Directions: Cut out the words and set them in the correct category.

raven	rabbit	milkman	pilgrim
husband	cattle	rodent	rival
pupil	bison	hero	chicken

Animals   People

Cognitive Flexibility
Category Sort #3
Animals vs. People

ANSWERS

Animals

rodent	cattle
chicken	bison
raven	rabbit

People

milkman	pilgrim
hero	rival
husband	pupil

Open

rodent	hero
raven	pupil
bison	rival

Closed

chicken	milkman
cattle	husband
rabbit	pilgrim

Cognitive Flexibility
Category Sort #4
Adjectives vs. Nouns

Directions: Cut out the words and set them in the correct category.

broken	little	jungle	insect
basket	splendid	fatal	radon
locust	noble	label	ample

Adjectives   Nouns

Cognitive Flexibility
Category Sort #4
Adjectives vs. Nouns

ANSWERS

Adjectives

fatal	splendid
ample	noble
broken	little

Nouns

locust	radon
label	basket
jungle	insect

Open

fatal	locust
broken	label
noble	jungle

Closed

ample	radon
splendid	basket
little	insect

Cognitive Flexibility

Category Sort #5
Adjectives vs. Things You Wear

Directions: Cut out the words and set them in the correct category.

bolo	jacket	humble	fickle
brittle	sandal	tunic	basic
brutal	tutu	potent	helmet

Adjectives   ## Things You Wear

Cognitive Flexibility
Category Sort #5
Adjectives vs. Things You Wear

ANSWERS

Adjectives

basic	brittle
brutal	potent
fickle	humble

Things You Wear

tunic	sandal
tutu	helmet
bolo	jacket

Open

basic	tutu
brutal	bolo
potent	tunic

Closed

fickle	sandal
brittle	helmet
humble	jacket

Cognitive Flexibility
Category Sort #6
I vs. E

Directions: Cut out the words and set them in the correct category.

crimat	miggle	kepton	jeblun
deggle	tinlit	bilux	remun
nepox	hibat	leple	lipdin

I   **E**

Cognitive Flexibility
Category Sort #6
I vs. E

ANSWERS

I

bilux	crimat
lipdin	miggle
tinlit	hibat

E

remun	jeblun
leple	deggle
kepton	nepox

Open

bilux	remun
crimat	leple
hibat	nepox

Closed

lipdin	kepton
tinlit	jeblun
miggle	deggle

Cognitive Flexibility
Category Sort #7
Adjectives vs. Sounds

Directions: Cut out the words and set them in the correct category.

vacant	frantic	rumble	jingle
rattle	simple	legal	music
bugle	final	siren	cosmic

Adjectives   Sounds

Cognitive Flexibility
Category Sort #7
Adjectives vs. Sounds

ANSWERS

Adjectives

vacant	simple
frantic	final
legal	cosmic

Sounds

bugle	music
siren	jingle
rumble	rattle

Open

vacant	legal
final	bugle
siren	music

Closed

simple	frantic
cosmic	rumble
rattle	jingle

Cognitive Flexibility
Category Sort #8
Plants vs. People

Directions: Cut out the words and set them in the correct category.

iris	fennel	bandit	dentist
uncle	cactus	lilac	student
human	tulip	pilot	crabgrass

Plants   People

Cognitive Flexibility
Category Sort #8
Plants vs. People

ANSWERS

Plants

cactus	tulip
crabgrass	lilac
iris	fennel

People

human	student
bandit	dentist
uncle	pilot

Open

tulip	pilot
lilac	student
iris	human

Closed

crabgrass	bandit
cactus	dentist
fennel	uncle

Multiple Classification Task

Start with the sorting activities on the previous two pages to prepare for the Multiple Classification Activity below. You will need a Boom™ Learning account to play the game online, or you may copy and cut out the words on the previous pages and use the 2x2 grid on page 139. You may sign up for a free Boom Account at www.wow.boomlearning.com. Additional CF activities are available there for a small additional charge. Strategies for students who need help with this task are below.

Example of the Multiple Classification Task.

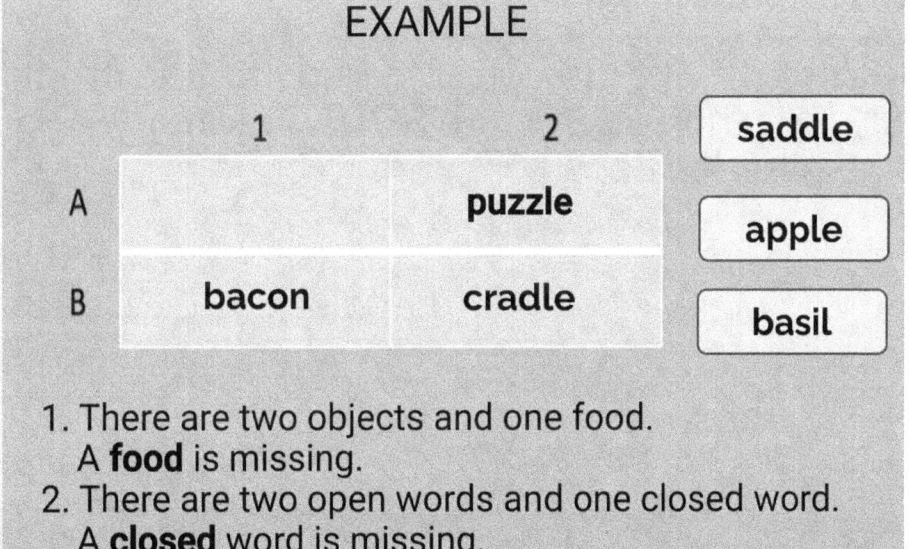

	1	2	
A		**puzzle**	saddle
B	**bacon**	**cradle**	apple
			basil

EXAMPLE

1. There are two objects and one food.
   A **food** is missing.
2. There are two open words and one closed word.
   A **closed** word is missing.
3. Look for a food that is closed.

Answer: apple

Multiple Classification Task

SODAS Strategy

S = Study
O = Observe
D = Deduce
A = Assess and Add
S = Select

Students who need more explicit instruction to be successful with the 2x2 matrix may benefit from the SODAS Strategy below.

EXAMPLE - Set the correct word into the empty box to complete the set. Use the **SODAS** strategy if you need help to decide which word to choose.

	1	2
A	pickle	saddle
B	basil	

bacon

sequin

puzzle

1. **Study** the words.

2. **Observe** that Row A contains 2 closed syllable words. Row B contains 1 open syllable word.

3. **Deduce** that Row B is missing an open syllable word.

4. Observe that column 1 contains 2 foods. Column 2 contains one object.

5. Deduce that Column 2 is missing an object.

6. **Assess and Add** the two missing elements. B2 needs to be an open syllable and an object.

7. **Select** a word that fits the pattern. **You may write down the 2 missing elements if that helps.**

Answer: sequin

Multiple Classification Activity
For Cognitive Flexibility

	1	2
A		
B		

MORPHOLOGY

INTRODUCTION

While phonemes represent the smallest units of sound, morphemes represent the smallest units of meaning. English is a morphophonemic language, which means that the phonemes and the morphological structure work together to influence how words are pronounced.

In her chapter on "Morphology for Reading, Spelling, and Vocabulary," in *Speech to Print: Language Essentials for Teachers* (Third Edition), Louisa Moats talks about the power of morphological awareness for building vocabulary. Being able to recognize morphemes enhances a student's ability to make reasonable inferences about a word's meaning in context. That recognition and understanding helps to "anchor a word in memory." In addition, we remember words best when we understand their relationship to other words.

Moats provides guidelines for morphology development and provides a scope and sequence for instruction based on the three layers of language: Anglo-Saxon, Latin, and Greek in that order. Using her framework, the examples found in *The Raven Remix* appear in **bold** below. As you choose morphology activities for your students, consider what they are ready to tackle in this sequence. Also, consider their decoding abilities and if they have been introduced previously to the affixes in this section. The activities are organized using Moats' scope and sequence.

Anglo-Saxon (common things and actions like *table, raven, cat, bee, jump, skip*)
1. Compound words like *tabletop, bumblebee.*
2. High-frequency prefixes added to Anglo-Saxon base words *(-*re, -*dis)* *remix*, *distress*
3. Common suffixes added to base words that do not cause spelling changes *(–s, -ed, -ing* in *cats, printed, swinging*)
4. Other suffixes that begin with a consonant *(-ment)*
5. Other suffixes that begin with a vowel (-**en, wooden*) Vowel suffixes that require changes in the base word because of the doubling, dropping, or changing rule (*en- hidden, bitten; -ed, -ing* in *slipped, stunning*).

Latin
1. Prefixes that end in a consonant or vowel-r (*con,*dis*) *contents, dismiss*
2. Prefixes that end in a vowel (**re*) added to Latin base elements *(relax, respect)*
3. Two-syllable prefixes (*intro*) *introduction*
4. Base elements such as *sist* (stand, make, be firm), *spect* (look, see)
5. Assimilated prefixes like *com* (from con) in *compel*; *as* (from ad) in *assist*.
6. Suffixes *(-ion) introduction*)

Greek
1. Combining forms such as *graph, auto, crypto, bio*

*Many Latin affixes such as **dis** and **re** are also used with Anglo-Saxon base words.

MORPHOLOGY

Continued (page 2)

Morpho Mania #1 – Compound Words
Create compound words to complete a fill-in-the-blank activity.

Morpho Mania #2: Suffix – ED shows that an action has happened in the past. It can sound like /əd/ (dented), /t/ (picked), or /d/ (filled). In this activity, students sort words containing suffix –ed based on the final sound. The focus on sound endings makes this activity a phonological exercise as well as a morphological one. If students have difficulty telling the difference between /t/ and /d/, they may benefit from discussing voiced versus unvoiced sounds. Prompt them to place a hand on their throat and feel the vibration of /d/. Notice how the /d/ and /t/ sounds are made the same way with the tongue tapping the roof of the mouth, except that /d/ is voiced. They can also study the letter just before suffix –ed. If that sound is voiced (/b/, /g/, /l/, /m/, /n/ /r/, /v/) then suffix –ed will be a voiced /d/. If the sound is unvoiced, (/k/, /f/, /p/, /sh/, /th/, /ch/) then suffix –ed will be an unvoiced /t/. If the final sound of a baseword is /d/ or /t/, then suffix –ed will have an added vowel sound - /əd/.

Morpho Mania #3: Suffix –EN is a vowel suffix because it starts with a vowel. This makes the base word subject to several spelling rules (doubling, dropping, changing). Some of the words chosen for this activity incorporate the doubling rule. Students should be able to read words following this rule even if they are not ready to spell them. Suffix –*en* affects meaning in several ways - a) changing a noun to an adjective – silk to silken, b) changing an adjective to a verb – glad to gladden, c) signifying that a verb is a past participle and that an action has been completed (was stolen). Past participles may also be used as adjectives (We found the stolen car.) Students can benefit from studying the words and definitions, even if they are not ready to study the various purposes of suffix –*en*.

Morpho Mania #4: Prefix RE means *again* or *back*. Students study the words containing the prefix RE and play a matching game. This is a very common prefix, so you may want to discuss other words containing RE that they use commonly, even if they are not yet able to read those words (*rewrite, repeat, restate, retire*). RE is a Latin prefix used with Latin bases, but it is also used with Anglo-Saxon bases. For older students, ask them to break into groups to research the etymology of the words in activity #4 using a source like etymonline.com. Have them make predictions about whether or not the base element for each word is Latin or Anglo-Saxon, and give reasons for their predictions before they look up these words. They won't find REMIX on etymonline.com because it is a newer term.

Morpho Mania #5-6 – Structured Word Inquiry: Students use a matrix to create a list of **word sums** for two different base elements *sist* and *spect.* Then they use words from each list to complete sentences or play matching games. Students will also use words from the **spect** matrix for writing a complex sentence in the Sentence Construction section.

MORPHOLOGY

Continued (page 3)

Both Word Matrices on the previous page were created with the Mini-Matrix Maker www.neilramsden.co.uk/spelling/matrix. The Word Matrix example to the right is also from that website.

un	**help** *"assistance"*	ful	ness
		less	ly ness

About the Word Matrix

1. A **Word Matrix** helps us explore word structure by organizing elements like **prefixes**, **base elements**, and **suffixes** into columns.
2. **Prefixes** are in the left column. **Base elements** are in the middle column. **Suffixes** are in the right columns.
3. A **Word Sum** is created by using one element from one column at a time to construct a word. You do not have to use an element from every column, but do not skip over columns.
4. Students will need the **Word Sums** to **Complete the Sentences** for activities 5-6.

Morpho Mania #7 - Greek Combining Element – *Graph* (writing, drawing**).** The words from this activity include *graphic, autograph, biography, biographer, autobiography, and cryptograph.* They come from the background section of *The Raven Remix.* This section is not decodable, but it may apply to older students reading at grade level.

Morpho Mania #8 – Etymology of Pluto, the Roman god of the underworld. It is the name of the cat in Poe's short story "The Black Cat."

REFERENCES
Bowers, P. (2009). *Teaching how the written word works: Using morphological problem-solving to develop students' language skills & engagement with the written word.* Ontario, Canada: Peter Bowers

Eggleston, R. L., Marks, R. A., Sun, X., Yu, L., Zhang, K., Nickerson, N., Hu, X., Caruso, V., & Kovelman, I. (2024). Lexical morphology as a source of risk and resilience for learning to read with dyslexia: An fNIRS investigation. *Journal of Speech, Language, and Hearing Research.* https://doi.org/23814764000300140072

Farrell, L.M., & Cushen-Whte, N. (2018). Structured literacy instruction. In J.R. Birsh & S. Carreker (Eds.) *Multisensory teaching of basic language skills* (4th ed., pp. 35-72). Baltimore, MD: Paul H. Brookes Publishing Co.

Moats, L.C. (2020). Speech to print: Language Essentials for Teachers. Baltimore, MD: Paul H. Brookes Publishing Co.

Quinion, M. (2008). Affixes: The building blocks of English. https://affixes.org/alpha/l/-le1.html

Ramsden, Neil. Mini Matrix Maker at www.neilramsden.co.uk/spelling/matrix

Morpho Mania #1
Compound Words

Directions: Draw lines to combine the words from columns 1 and 2 to create compound words. Then match them to the definitions below.

1	2
table	in
bumble	top
with	not
up	bee
can	set

1. He set the dish on the _____.

2. Is that a _____ that stung him

3. Look _____ the chest.

4. Did the cat _____ the kid?

5. He _____ catch the bug.

Morpho Mania #1
Compound Words

ANSWERS

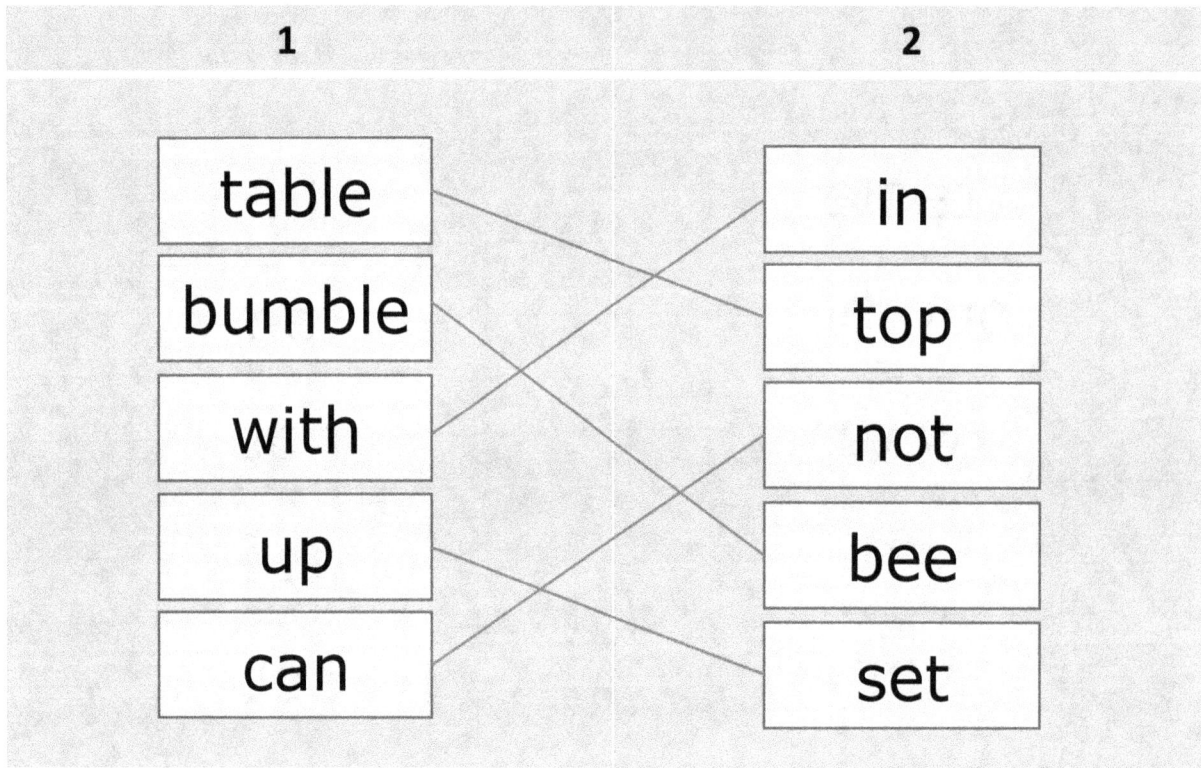

1	2
table	in
bumble	top
with	not
up	bee
can	set

1. He set the dish on the - **tabletop**

2. Is that a **bumblebee** that stung him?

3. Look **within** the chest.

4. Did the cat **upset** the kid?

5. He **cannot** catch the bug.

Morpho Mania #2
Suffix *-ed*
based on *The Raven Remix*
by Carolee Dean

Suffix -ed tells us that an action has happened in the past. It can sound like /ed/, /d/, or /t/. Cut out the words at the bottom and place them in the correct category. Use the word cards from the front of the book for more options.

/əd/	/d/	/t/

ended	filled	picked	printed
grinned	dented	yelled	stuffed
crashed	passed	drifted	stunned

145

Morpho Mania #2
Suffix -ed
based on *The Raven Remix*
by Carolee Dean

ANSWERS

/ed/	/d/	/t/
ended	grinned	crashed
dented	filled	picked
drifted	yelled	passed
printed	stunned	stuffed

Morpho Mania #3
Suffix -en

based on *The Raven Remix*
by Carolee Dean

-en is a Latin suffix that has several functions including:
1)   Changing a noun to an adjective – *wood to wooden*
2)   Signifying that an action has been completed (*bite to bitten*)
3)   Changing a verb into an adjective – *broke* to *broken, wove* to *woven, hide* to *hidden*

Directions: Study the words and their meanings. Then make cards for the Morpho Mania Memory Game.

Word	Meaning
wooden	Made of wood. Ex: The vest was in the <u>wooden</u> chest.
bitten	Related to bite. Ex. Was he <u>bitten</u> by the cat?
broken	Torn or shattered. Ex. The <u>broken</u> bug landed on the vellum sheet.
hidden	Concealed or covered Ex. He left the cash in a <u>hidden</u> spot.
woven	Made of interlaced threads. Ex. The chest held <u>woven</u> baskets.

Morpho Mania #3
Memory Game
Suffix -en

Memory Game Cards – Cut out the terms, paste onto game cards, turn upside down, and shuffle to play the memory game. Each player turns over two cards at a time to match the words to their meanings.

wooden	Related to bite.
bitten	Torn or shattered.
broken	Made of wood.
hidden	Made of interlaced threads.
woven	Concealed or covered.

Morpho Mania #3
Prefix *re*
based on *The Raven Remix*
by Carolee Dean

re is a Latin prefix that means **back** or **again**.
Directions:
1. Study the words and their meanings.
2. Make cards for the Morpho Mania Memory Game.
3. Talk about other words you know that start with the prefix **re**

Word	Meaning
remix	something mixed **again** - a new version of an old song, book, or poem. Ex: The Raven <u>Remix</u> is based on a poem by Poe.
relax	to sit **back** or loosen **again**. Ex. He needs to loosen up and <u>relax</u>.
regret	to look **back** with sadness Ex. Did he <u>regret</u> skipping school?
request	to ask for something or question **again** Ex. They looked for the chest at Kidd's <u>request</u>.
retelling	a story told **again**. Ex. Many people have created **retellings** of Poe's stories.
respect	to look **back** at someone with high regard. Ex. Theater critics <u>respected</u> Poe's mother, but not his father.

Morpho Mania #4
Memory Game
Prefix re

Memory Game Cards – Cut out the terms, paste onto game cards, turn upside down, and shuffle to play the memory game. Each player turns over two cards at a time to match the words to their meanings.

remix	to sit **back** or loosen **again**
relax	something mixed **again**
regret	to look **back** at someone with high regard
request	a story told **again**
retelling	to ask for something or question **again**
respect	to look **back** with sadness

Morpho Mania #5
Structured Word Inquiry
Word Sums for SIST

Directions: Use the matrix below to create as many word sums as possible. The first one is done for you.

Created with *Mini Matrix-Maker*, at www.neilramsden.co.uk/spelling/matrix

1._____insisted_____
2._____
3._____
4._____
5._____
6._____
7._____
8._____

Morpho Mania #5
Structured Word Inquiry
Sentences for SIST

Use the words below to complete the sentences. The first one is done for you. See Morpho Mania #5 for definitions.

insisted
consisted
resist
assisted
assistant
inconsistent

Example: The weather can be very **in + con + sist + ent.**

1. The kid ____+_____+____ that he needed to go back to class.

2. He could not ___+_____ the table full of snacks.

3. The muffins ____+_____+____ of apples, nuts, and seeds.

4. The man needed an ____+_____+_____ to help him.

5. The kid ____+_____+_____ the man and helped him find the chest of cash.

ANSWERS

1. The kid **in + sist + ed** that he needed to go back to class.

2. He could not **re + sist** the table full of snacks.

3. The muffins **con + sist + ed** of apples, nuts, and seeds.

4. The man needed an **as + sist + ant** to help him.

5. The kid **as + sist + ed** the man and helped him find the chest of cash.

Morpho Mania #5
based on the background section of
The Raven Remix
by Carolee Dean

Latin Base Element **SIST**: **stand, take a stand, be firm, make**

Study how the base element *sist* is used in the words below.
Then print the matching game on the next page.

Word	Meaning
insist	demand, **stand** upon -(verb) Mom *insisted* that I pick up my socks.
consist	to be **made** of things that **stand** or stay together -(verb) The cake *consisted* of flour, water, and sugar.
consistent	stable, **standing** firm -(adjective) A person who always tells the truth is *consistent*.
inconsistent	unstable, not **standing** firm -(adjective) The weather can be very *inconsistent*.
resist	to oppose or **stand** against -(verb) I cannot *resist* eating apple pie.
resistant	the quality of **standing** against something -(adjective) That fabric is fire-*resistant*.
assist	to help or **stand** by -(verb) How can I *assist* you?
assistant	a person who helps or **stands** by -(noun) Her *assistant* got her coffee every morning.

Morpho Mania #5
Memory Game
Base - SIST

Memory Game Cards – Cut out the cards, paste onto construction paper, turn upside down, and shuffle to play the memory game. Each player turns over two cards at a time to match the words to their meanings.

insist	resistant	stable, **standing** firm
consist	assist	unstable, not **standing** firm
consistent	assistant	to be **made** of things that **stand** or stay together
inconsistent	demand, **stand** upon	to oppose or **stand** against
resist	to help or **stand** by	**standing** against something
	a person who helps or **stands** by	

Morpho Mania #6A
Structured Word Inquiry
Word Sums for SPECT

Directions: Use the matrix below to create as many word sums as possible. The first one is done for you.

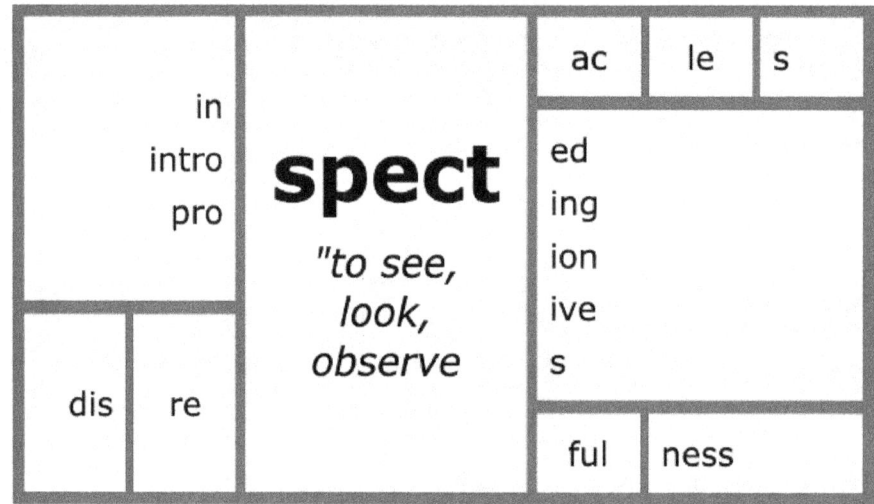

Created with *Mini Matrix-Maker*, at www.neilramsden.co.uk/spelling/matrix

1._____inspected_____

2._____

3._____

4._____

5._____

6._____

7._____

Directions: Use the matrix below to create as many word sums as possible. The first one is done for you.

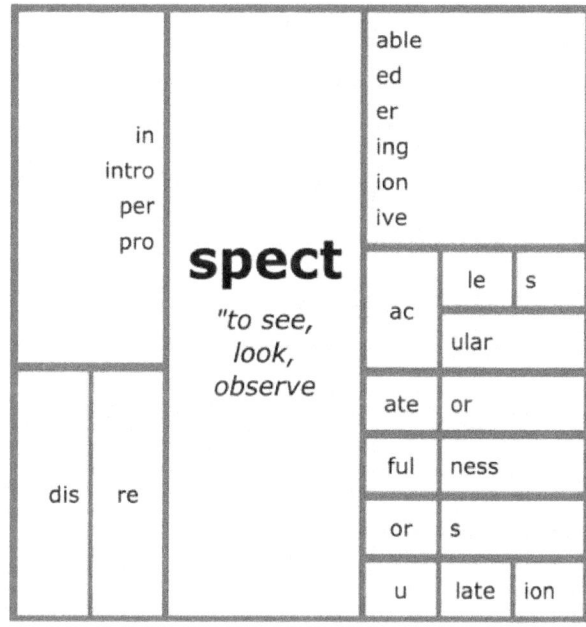

Created with *Mini Matrix-Maker*, at www.neilramsden.co.uk/spelling/matrix

1._____ inspected _____

2._____

3._____

4._____

5._____

6._____

7._____

Use the words below to complete the sentences. The first one is done for you.

inspect
inspection
spectacles
respect
prospects
disrespectful

Example: Do not be **dis + re + spect + ful** to your dad.

1. The man had three good ____+_____+__ for a job.

2. I cannot ___+_____ a vandal.

3. The detective will ___ + _____ the stolen van.

4. The man cannot see without his ____+_____+_____ + ___

5. Did the shop pass the ____+_____+_____?

ANSWERS

1. The man had three good **pro + spect + s** for a job.

2. I cannot **re + spect** a vandal.

3. The detective will **in + spect** the stolen van.

4. The man cannot see without his **spect + ac + le + s**.

5. Did the shop pass the **in + spect + ion**?

Morpho Mania #6
based on the background section of
The Raven Remix
by Carolee Dean

Latin Base Element **SPECT**: **to see, look, observe**

Study how the base element *spect* is used in the words below.
Then print the matching game on the next page.

Word	Meaning
inspect	to **look** within -(verb) Mom *inspected* my backpack.
disrespect	to **look** back at someone with low regard. -(noun) Theater critics treated Poe's father with <u>disrespect</u>.
spectacle	an event to watch or **see** -(noun) The football game will be a public spectacle.
prospect	something to **see** or work for in the future -(noun) Poe had some good prospects for his future.
specter	a ghost – something that is **seen** -(noun) The <u>specter</u> looked like a sheet.

Morpho Mania #6
Memory Game
Base Element *SPECT*

Memory Game Cards – Cut out the terms, paste onto game cards, turn upside down, and shuffle to play the memory game. Each player turns over two cards at a time to match the words to their meanings.

inspect	something to **see** or work for in the future
disrespect	to **look** back at someone with low regard
spectacle	an event to watch or **see**
prospect	a ghost – something that is **seen**
specter	to **look** within

Morpho Mania #7
based on the background section of
The Raven Remix
by Carolee Dean

Greek Base Element **GRAPH**: **writing, drawing**

Study how the base element *graph* is used in the words below.
Then print the matching game on the next page.

Word	Meaning
graphic	Vivid **writing**. -(adjective) Many of Poe's stories are too graphic for young children.
autograph	A signature **written** with one's own hand. -(noun) He gave his fans his *autograph*.
biography	The **written** story of another person's life. -(noun). *Midnight Dreary* is a *biography* written about Poe's death.
biographer	A person who **writes** someone else's life story. -(noun) Several different *biographers* wrote about the life of Poe.
autobiography	The story of a person's life **written** by that person. -(noun) Did Poe write his own *autobiography*?
cryptograph	Something **written** in a secret code. -(noun) Did he solve the *cryptograph*?

Morpho Mania #7
Memory Game
based on *The Raven Remix*
by Carolee Dean

Memory Game Cards – Cut out the cards, paste onto construction paper, turn upside down, and shuffle to play the memory game. Each player turns over two cards at a time to match the words to their meanings.

graphic	The **written** story of another person's life
autograph	Vivid **writing**
biography	Something **written** in a secret code.
biographer	The story of a person's life **written** by that person.
autobiography	A signature **written** with one's own hand.
cryptography	A person who **writes** the story of someone else's life.

Pluto was the Roman god of the underworld, although Pluto actually means the "god of wealth." Pluto comes from the Latin word, *ploutos* which means "wealth" or "overflowing." It seems odd to think about the god of the underworld as the god of wealth, but many valuable things come from underground such as gold, silver, and precious stones.

The feline who comes back from the dead in Edgar Allan Poe's story "The Black Cat" is named **Pluto**. The creepy cat in *The Raven Remix* has the same name.

In his poem "The Raven" Poe tells the bird, "Get thee back into the tempest and the night's **Plutonian** shore."

The "Plutonion shore" refers to the shore of the River Styx, the boundary between earth and the underworld. Poe is telling the bird to go back to the underworld.

Other References to Pluto

Pluto was long considered to be the ninth planet from our sun. It was reclassified as a dwarf planet because it was not large enough to dominate its orbital path. Pluto got its name because it was dark, cold, and far away.

Plutonium was a metal (element 94) discovered in 1942. It was named after the planet Pluto when Pluto was still considered a planet. Uranium (element 92) was named after the planet Uranus. Neptunium (element 93) was named after the planet Neptune.

Plutocracy refers to a society where the rich have all the power.

VOCABULARY & SEMANTICS

INTRODUCTION

Vocabulary is a foundational building block of both listening and reading comprehension, but it can be challenging to include robust vocabulary when focusing on limited syllable types. On the other hand, even the most basic word forms can provide opportunities for exploring advanced vocabulary, especially when multi-syllable words are included. When vocabulary is content-rich and comes from material related to the curriculum, repeated exposure to words is more natural. Read about vocabulary on the page for <u>COR Instruction</u> on the website.

The Raven Remix does NOT have multi-syllable words divided into syllables as you may have seen done in the Levels 1 and 2 activity books. However, if your student still needs work on this concept, they can use the word cards and place a slash (/) between syllables to prepare for practice reading the words.

Pre-teach new words before students are asked to read them in context. It can also be helpful to teach students strategies for determining the meaning of new words on their own by looking at the context **before** they are told the definition. Students with dyslexia need even more exposure to a word than their peers, so if they have already been introduced to a word, it is still helpful to explore the word in context. Context is especially important for understanding multiple-meaning words.

Rereading helps students develop confidence and fluency, but there needs to be a meaningful reason for rereading a text. Ask students to reread the story to find multi-meaning words and to decide which meaning of the word applies to the story.

References:
Wright, T.S., & Neuman, S.B. (2015). The power of content-rich vocabulary instruction. *Perspectives on Language and Literacy*, 41 (3), 25-28.

Shanahan, T. (2015). Are you lactating? On the importance of academic language. *Perspectives on Language and Literacy, 41*(3), 14-16.

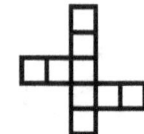

ACTIVITIES

Word Clues – Seek and Find: Sometimes the meaning of a new word is stated directly within the context of a nearby sentence. In this activity, students underline the definition that is provided in the context.

Multiple Meaning Match Up – Match words in a memory game to explore double meanings.

The Cat's Meow – Match meanings to phrases and idioms to explore figurative language about cats in Catty Idioms and Feline Phrases. See the Alphabet Code Breaker activities at the beginning of the book to find more fun activities using these idioms.

WOW (Wonder of Words) Vocabulary: The vocabulary word lists may be used for a variety of games listed below. Students with dyslexia may need some of the definitions read aloud. Instruct students to divide the words if needed. Words are from the story poem. A blank Vocabulary Template and blank Vocabulary Foldable have been provided for students who are ready to tackle the additional words and definitions not listed here from the Background Information section of The Raven Remix. These words may be found in the vocabulary section of the chapter book.

Games & Activities for WOW

1. **Alphabet** – Cut out the words and put them in alphabetical order.

2. **Vocabulary Foldable** – Follow the directions to complete a vocabulary foldable.

3. **Memory Game** – Make two copies of the words. Glue them onto construction paper and play the Memory Game by turning the cards face down. Pick two at a time, looking for a match. Read the words out loud as you turn them over and give the meaning. Start with 5 sets of words. When that is manageable, go up to 6, then 7, then 8 or more.

4. **Go Fish** –Make two sets of cards and play Go Fish.

Word Clues
Seek and Find
based on *The Raven Remix*
by Carolee Dean

DIRECTIONS: Read the word in the left column. Find it in the sentence and circle it. Then underline the information that helps you understand the meaning of the word.

Word	Meaning
pitch	The cat was as black as pitch, the sticky tar used for roofing.
spent	After an afternoon at the inn, the boy was spent and worn out.
relish	Ed relished helping students. It was something he greatly enjoyed.
vellum	The bug fell on a sheet of vellum; a calfskin used for writing.
fragment	It was a fragment of cloth, just a small piece.
mutant	That cat looks like a mutant. It's not normal at all.
ample	It was an ample chest, big enough to hold all the treasure.
pendulum	The pendulum was next to the pit. The swinging lever almost hit the rat.
topaz	The chest was filled with topaz and other gemstones.
bolo	He wore a bolo around his neck instead of a tie.

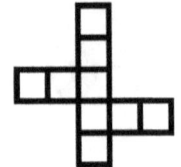

Word Clues
Seek and Find
based on *The Raven Remix*
by Carolee Dean

ANSWERS

Word	Meaning
pitch	The cat was as black as pitch, the (sticky tar) used for roofing.
spent	After an afternoon at the inn, the boy was spent and (worn out.)
relish	Ed relished helping students. It was something he greatly (enjoyed.)
vellum	The bug fell on a sheet of vellum; a (calfskin) used for writing.
fragment	It was a fragment of cloth, just a (small piece.)
mutant	That cat looks like a mutant. It's (not) (normal) at all.
ample	It was an ample chest, (big enough) to hold all the treasure.
pendulum	The pendulum was next to the pit. The (swinging lever) almost hit the rat.
topaz	The chest was filled with topaz and other (gemstones.)
bolo	He (wore) a bolo (around his neck) instead of a tie.

Multiple Meaning Match Up
based on *The Raven Remix*
by Carolee Dean

Directions: 1. Make two copies of the words below.
2 Cut out the words and glue them onto construction paper.
3. Play the Memory Matching game.
4. Make sure you choose words with the same meanings.

relish a food made of pickles	**relish** enjoy	
pitch to throw	**pitch** a solid form of tar	**spent** tired, worn out
ring finger jewelry	**ring** the sound a bell makes	**spent** paid money
pen a small area for animals	**pen** writing instrument	**pit** a hole in the ground
chest trunk of the body	**chest** a box	**pit** the stone in the middle of a fruit

The Cat's Meow #1
Feline Phrases
based on *The Raven Remix*
by Carolee Dean

Directions:
1. Study the phrases and their meanings.
2. Play a matching game with the words on the next page.

Feline Phrases

Scaredy cat – a coward or timid person.
Cats tend to overreact when frightened by small things. They may jump, run, and hide.
That scaredy cat won't join the track team because he is afraid he will lose the race.

Catnap – A short nap in the middle of the day.
Cats tend to take several short naps during the day.
He was able to finish his homework after a short catnap.

Cat burglar – A very quiet thief.
A thief who can enter and leave a house without being noticed is called a cat burglar. Cats are so quiet that you sometimes don't know they are there. They can also be very sneaky.
The cat burglar got away before we knew anything was missing.

Copycat – A person who imitates someone else.
Cats sometimes imitate each other.
He got tired of his little brother being a copycat.

The cat's meow – Something very desirable.
Cats often meow when they want something.
His new car was the cat's meow.

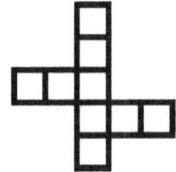

The Cat's Meow #1
Memory Game
based on *The Raven Remix*
by Carolee Dean

Memory Game Cards – Cut out the cards, paste onto construction paper, turn upside down, and shuffle to play the memory game. Each player turns over two cards at a time to match the idioms to their meanings.

Scaredy cat	a coward or timid person
catnap	a short nap in the middle of the day
Cat burglar	A very quiet thief
copycat	A person who imitates someone else
The cat's meow	Something very desirable

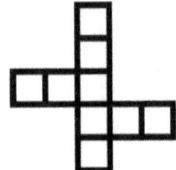

The Cat's Meow #2
Catty Idioms
based on *The Raven Remix*
by Carolee Dean

Directions:
1. Study the idioms and their meanings.
2. Play a matching game with the words on the next page.

Feline Idioms

Don't let the cat out of the bag. – Don't ruin the surprise.
This saying may date back to a time when merchants would sell baby pigs to customers and put them in a sack so they would be easier to carry. Sometimes, they put a cat inside instead because they were less valuable than pigs. When the new owner got home, they let out the cat and got an unpleasant surprise.
Bill's birthday party is a surprise, so don't let the cat out of the bag.

It's raining cats and dogs. – A bad rainstorm.
This saying may have started in London. Many stray animals roamed the streets of London in the 17th century. During heavy rain, cats and dogs might be seen floating down the street.
You'd better take an umbrella. It's raining cats and dogs.

What the cat dragged in - Someone dressed in a dirty or messy way.
Cats often bring small animals like birds or mice home for their owners. If your cat drags a tiny mouse into the house, it will look like a mess. It would be an unpleasant surprise.
I need a shower. I feel like something the cat dragged in.

Curiosity killed the cat. – If you are too nosy, you may regret it.
Cats are inquisitive, and sometimes that gets them into trouble.
Sue found her aunt's secret cookie recipe and discovered why curiosity killed the cat when she learned what was in the dessert.

It's like herding cats. – Organizing a group of people can be difficult.
The phrase may have been first used in the Monty Python film, *The Life of Brian*. It's easy to herd cows and sheep, but it would be impossible to herd cats.
Trying to get the other students to help with the history project was like herding cats.

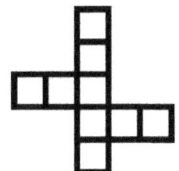

The Cat's Meow #2
Memory Game
based on *The Raven Remix*
by Carolee Dean

Memory Game Cards – Cut out the cards, paste onto construction paper, turn upside down, and shuffle to play the memory game. Each player turns over two cards at a time to match the idioms to their meanings.

Don't let the cat out of the bag.	Don't ruin the surprise.
It's raining cats and dogs.	It's a bad rainstorm.
What the cat dragged in.	Someone dressed in a dirty or messy way.
Curiosity killed the cat.	If you are nosy, you may regret it.
It's like herding cats.	Organizing a group of people can be difficult.

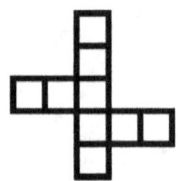

WOW Vocabulary #1
based on *The Raven Remix*
by Carolee Dean

1. Study the words below.
2. Use them to make a vocabulary foldable.

Word	Meaning
ample	plentiful, enough
banshee	a screaming phantom woman
bolo	a type of western necktie
cask	a barrel for holding liquids
chimpanzee	a type of ape
compel	to force or push toward action
crimson	deep red
cunning	tricky

WOW Vocabulary #2
based on *The Raven Remix*
by Carolee Dean

1. Study the words below.
2. Use them to make a vocabulary foldable.

Word	Meaning
flee	run away
fleet	swift, rapid
fragment	a piece or scrap
gibbon	a type of small ape
hubbub	confusing noise
hulking	heavy and bulky
inn	a small hotel
intent	decided or resolved

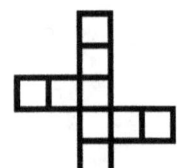

WOW Vocabulary #3
based on *The Raven Remix*
by Carolee Dean

1. Study the words below.
2. Use them to make a vocabulary foldable.

Word	Meaning
locket	part of a necklace
locust	a type of grasshopper
mammoth	huge
mandrill	a large baboon
mantel	a shelf above a fireplace
mutant	an animal that is malformed.
oblong	oval
opal	a multi-colored precious gemstone

WOW Vocabulary #4
based on *The Raven Remix*
by Carolee Dean

1. Study the 2-syllable words below.
2. Use them to make a vocabulary foldable.

Word	Meaning
pedigree	lineage or ancestry
prudent	wise
putrid	rotten
quelled	silenced or stopped
racking	sharp and sudden
regret	feeling sorry
relish	enjoy
request	ask for something

WOW Vocabulary #5
based on *The Raven Remix*
by Carolee Dean

1. Study the 2-syllable words below.
2. Use them to make a vocabulary foldable.

Word	Meaning
ruckus	loud disturbance
script	letters used in writing
seek	look or search
sequined	covered in small shiny disks
settle	to rest
sill	a wooden plan at a window or door
socket	a hollow place that holds something
spent	tired

WOW Vocabulary #6
based on *The Raven Remix*
by Carolee Dean

1. Study the words below.
2. Use them to make a vocabulary foldable.

Word	Meaning
spiral	shaped like a coil
splendid	rich and grand
stash	something that his hidden
stock	fill
strudel	a fruit pastry
stunning	astonishing beauty
sullen	gloomy
topaz	a semiprecious gemstone

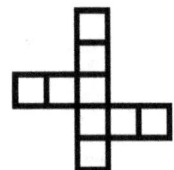

WOW Vocabulary #7
based on *The Raven Remix*
by Carolee Dean

1. Study the list below.
2. Use them to make a vocabulary foldable.

Word	Meaning
trinket	a small piece of jewelry
tufted	having clumps of feathers or hair
vanish	disappear
vellum	a calfskin used as a writing surface
velvet	a thick, soft fabric

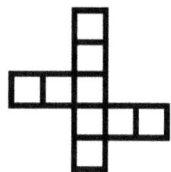

WOW Vocabulary Template
Blank

1. Find words from the Background Section of *The Raven Remix* and write them in the left column.
2. Write the MEANING in the right column.
3. Use the words to make a vocabulary foldable.

Word	Meaning

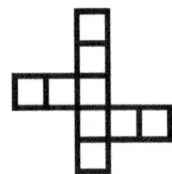

Vocabulary Foldable
Example

Directions:
1. Write (or cut and paste) 8 words from the WOW Vocabulary List on a blank vocabulary foldable.

2. Then cut on the dotted lines between the words.

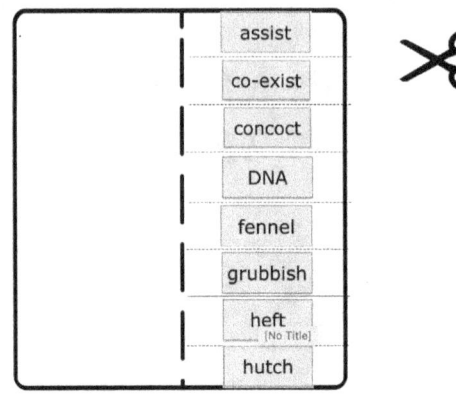

3. Fold the paper in half lengthwise.

4. Open the foldable and write (or paste) definitions for the words on the inside on the right. Draw pictures to go with the word on the left.

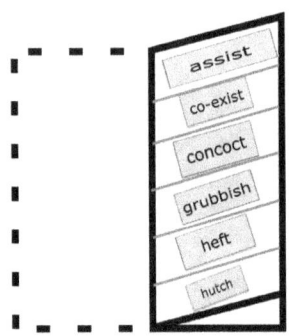

5. Close the foldable. Test yourself by reading a word out loud. Say the definition. Then open the foldable and see if you were right.

6. When you are done studying the words and definitions cut them apart, glue them onto construction paper, and play a memory matching game.

.

Vocabulary Foldable
Blank

SENTENCE CONSTRUCTION (pg. 1)

All that is needed for a complete sentence is a *Subject* (the Doer) and a Predicate (What is being Done). We will use examples from Poe's short story "The Purloined Letter" to illustrate how to expand a sentence by asking a series of WH- Questions. Share the explanations below with your students to the degree that they are ready for the concepts. The summary below is taken from the background section of *The Raven Remix: A Mashup of Poe Titles.*

"The Purloined Letter" Summary

Mr. D. steals a letter from a woman with a high-ranking government position. Then, he blackmails her to get her to agree to his political demands. She does not want her letter's contents revealed, so she is afraid she must go along with his schemes.

The police search Mr. D.'s home but cannot find the letter. They ask C. Auguste Dupin for help. Dupin studies Mr. D. and concludes that he would have hidden the letter in plain sight. He visits the man's home and sees the letter in a rack with other correspondences. He observes that it has been disguised to look like a letter from someone else. Dupin notes its appearance, goes home, and creates a duplicate.

The next time he visits Mr. D., Dupin swaps out the two letters. He later gives the stolen letter to the police.

Simple Sentence: Mr. D.   **hid.**   **(This could technically be a complete sentence,**
                subject   predicate   **but it needs more information to make sense.)**

What did he hide? This question requires adding a direct object – *the letter.*
            Mr. D. hid **the letter.**

Which letter did he hide? A variety of adjectives are possible: *private, secret, purloined. Purloin* is a verb meaning *to steal.* Sometimes, verbs act like adjectives. Students may mistake these adjectives for the predicate because they sound like verbs. In the sentence below, notice that "hid" is still the main action of the sentence.
            Mr. D. hid the **purloined** letter.

Which questions can also result in a relative clause that describes the subject. Relative clauses start with relative pronouns such as *who, whoever, whom, whomever, that, which, when, where, whose.*
            Mr. D., **who thought he could blackmail a high-**
            ranking government official, hid the purloined letter.

SENTENCE CONSTRUCTION (pg. 2)

In the sentence on the previous page, notice the distance between the subject (Mr. D.) and the predicate (hid). The more distance there is between the subject and the predicate, the more likely it is that students will misinterpret the sentence, especially since another clause has been added with a new subject (who) and a new predicate (thought). Furthermore, another character (the government official) is included.

Where did Mr. D. hide the letter? Phrases that start with prepositions such as *in, on, under, around* are called prepositional phrases.

> Mr. D., who thought he could blackmail a high-ranking government official, hid the purloined letter **in plain sight in a letter rack.**

How did Mr. D. hide the letter? Students can answer this question by adding adverbs such as *cleverly, secretly,* or *quietly* or by adding an entire clause that functions like an adverb, which we will talk about next.

> Mr. D., who thought he could blackmail a high-ranking government official, **cleverly** hid the purloined letter in plain sight on a card rack.

When did Mr. D. hide the letter? Subordinating conjunctions that deal with time are called temporal subordinating conjunctions, words like *when, while, before, after, until, once, as soon as.* They may be used to introduce clauses. Clauses have their own subject and predicate. When these clauses modify the verb (to give us information about **when** something is happening), they function as an adverb and are called adverbial clauses, providing us more information about **How**. "After he stole it" is a clause. Without both a subject and a predicate, the information would be an adverbial phrase "after stealing it."

> Mr. D., who thought he could blackmail a high-ranking government official, cleverly hid the purloined letter in plain sight on a card rack **after he stole it.**

Why did Mr. D. hide the letter, or why did he do it in that manner? A subordinating conjunction that introduces a clause of reason or purpose is called a causal conjunction. These include words like *because, since,* and *so that.* These clauses are also adverbial clauses because they give us more information about the action.

> Mr. D., who thought he could blackmail a high-ranking government official, cleverly hid the purloined letter in plain sight on a card rack after he stole it **because he knew the police would not expect it to be out in the open.**

The basic sentence in its simple form is still **Mr. D. hid the letter.** Understanding the function of the various clauses and phrases helps us figure out the basic action of the sentence.

SENTENCE CONSTRUCTION (pg. 3)

Mystery writers are experts at hiding clues in plain sight. Have you ever watched a mystery movie? When you got to the end, did you remember a clue that was obvious but didn't seem important earlier in the story?

Now it's your turn to create a sentence with your students where you will hide essential information by adding phrases and clauses. Start with a simple sentence telling **who** did **what**. Create your own or use one of the examples below. Display the sentence on a Whiteboard or Smartboard.

1. *The detective lost the evidence.*
2. *The secretary stole the money.*
3. *Mary broke the vase.*

Next, ask your students to help you add phrases and clauses to expand the sentence. The sentence will be more interesting, but it will also be more challenging for other people to figure out the subject and predicate.

Use questions like the ones below:
1. **Which** person is the subject (the tall one, the intelligent one, the one who always wore a strange hat?)
2. **Where** does the action happen? (in a haunted house, under a bridge)
3. **How** does it happen? (silently, secretly)
4. **When** does it happen? (during lunch, while everyone else was on vacation)
5. **Why** did it happen? (because....)

This sentence is most mysterious!

Sometimes, it takes a bit of investigating to figure out the Simple Subject (Doer) and the Simple Predicate (What is being Done). The information may be hidden in plain sight, like a purloined letter. Students must become Sentence Sleuths like Poe's amateur detective Dupin. The activities described on the next pages were designed to help students understand the underlying structure of sentences, with the easier activities coming first and building in complexity.

SENTENCE CONSTRUCTION (pg. 4)

Sentence Construction #1: Identifying Complete Sentences (The Doer and the Doing) – Students underline the simple subject and circle the simple predicate to help determine if the sentence is complete or incomplete. If it is incomplete, they identify what is missing.

Sentence Construction #2: Compound Subjects and Predicates – Simple sentences may contain two or more subjects or predicates. In this activity, students determine if a sentence contains a compound subject, a compound predicate, or neither. Be aware that simply having a compound subject or predicate does not make the sentence compound.

Sentence Construction #3: Direct Objects – The direct object receives the action. A sentence does not need a direct object to be complete, but a direct object can add essential information. In this activity, students fill in the blank with a direct object (or objects) to complete the sentences.

Sentence Construction #4: Sentence Combining – Students combine two simple sentences using a coordinating conjunction. Give the COORDINATING CONJUNCTIONS graphic to students as you explain this concept. Allow them to reference it as they complete the activity. If both sides of the resulting sentence contain a subject and a predicate, the result is a COMPOUND SENTENCE. If not, it is a simple sentence.

Coordinating junctions can be remembered by the term FANBOYS (*for, and, nor, but, or, yet, so*). Be aware that *so* is tricky because it can serve as either a coordinating conjunction (*and so*) or a subordinating conjunction (*so that*).

Punctuation: Use a comma before coordinating conjunctions joining two clauses only if both contain a subject and a predicate:

> The boy walked into the inn, and he went on an adventure.   COMPOUND
> The boy walked into the inn and went on an adventure.   SIMPLE

The subject "he" is missing from the second example. Because the second part of this sentence lacks a subject, it is simple.

Sentence Construction #5: Phrases and Clauses – Students determine if a string of words is a phrase or a clause. Both are groups of words, but a clause contains a subject **and** a predicate. A clause may or may not be a complete sentence. A phrase is never a complete sentence even if it is long (i.e. *underneath the bright and radiant glowing harvest moon*).

while he was waiting (clause)
She went to the store. (clause)
below the old bridge on the edge of town (phrase)

SENTENCE CONSTRUCTION (pg. 5)

Sentence Construction #6: Dependent and Independent Clauses – Students determine if clauses are independent (can stand alone as a sentence) or dependent (do NOT express a complete thought on their own). Give the SUBORDINATING CONJUNCTIONS graphic to students as you explain this concept. Dependent clauses often start with a subordinating conjunction (*because, since, although, after, when* etc.). When both a dependent and an independent clause appear in one sentence, it is a COMPLEX SENTENCE. See below:

The young man ran from the inn (independent clause)
because he was frightened by the animals (dependent clause)

Sentence Construction #7: Where Things Happen: Students analyze sentences to find prepositional phrases. Remind students that adding a phrase to a sentence makes it longer and more interesting, but it does not by itself result in a complex or compound sentence. The following example is still a simple sentence: *The black cat hid under the table.*

Sentence Construction #8: Sentence Flips for "Where" – Students work with sentences that have been flipped so that the prepositional phrase comes first. These types of sentences can be confusing for students because the Doer and the Doing come later in the sentence. *Under the table, the black cat hid.*

Sentence Construction #9: When Things Happen – Students analyze sentences to find temporal "when" statements. *He left the inn after lunch.*

Sentence Construction #10: Sentence Flips for "When" – Students work with sentences that have been flipped so that the temporal "when" statement comes first. *After lunch, he left the inn.*

Sentence Construction #11: Why Things Happen (A Clause with a Cause) – Students work with the terms *because, and since* to create clauses of reason. *He had a snack because he was hungry.*

Sentence Construction #12: Sentence Flips for "Why" - Students create flipped sentences that begin with subordinating conjunctions. *Because he was hungry, he had a snack.*

Sentence Construction #13: Who is Doing What? - Pick an illustration from the book. Give students the Wh-Questions Icons page along with this worksheet. Have them describe what is going on in the illustration by answering the WH questions. They then use their answers to construct one long, complex sentence.

SENTENCE CONSTRUCTION (pg. 6)

Sentence Construction #14: Sentence Quest – This multi-step activity spans morphology, sentence structure, and paragraph writing. First, students generate a list of words from the **SPECTER** activity in the Morphology section. Then, they choose an image to write about. Next, they ask a series of WH Questions about the image to construct a complex sentence using **SPECTER** words.. Finally, they use that sentence to start a story.

Sentence Construction #15: Just for Fun: Hiding Whodunnit – The more distance there is between the subject and the predicate, the more difficult it is to understand who is doing what. In this activity, the student takes a simple sentence related to the story of "The Purloined Letter" and purposefully *hides* the identity of the guilty party by adding as many phrases and clauses as possible to the sentence. Please point out that this is NOT a good way to write when we want our communication to be clear and to the point. It is an exercise in exaggeration.

References:

Hochman, J.C. & MacDermott-Duffy, B. (2018). Composition: Evidence-based instruction. In J.R. Birsh & S. Carreker (Eds.) Multisensory teaching of basic language skills (4th ed., pp. 205-253. Baltimore, MD: Paul H. Brookes Publishing Co.

Nelson, N.W. (2013). Syntax development in the school-age years: implications for assessment and intervention. *Perspectives on Language and Literacy*. 39 (3), 9-15.

Van Cleave, W. (2014). *Writing matters: Developing sentence skills in students of all ages (Second Edition).* Greenville, SC: W.V.C.ED

Glossary of SENTENCE Terms

Phrase – A group of words that may or may not include a subject **or** a predicate, but not both.

Clause – A group of words that includes a subject **and** a predicate.

Independent Clause – Contains a subject **and** a predicate. Can stand alone as a sentence.

Dependent Clause – Contains a subject **and** a predicate but needs an independent clause to make sense.

Simple Sentence – One independent clause with a subject and a predicate that forms a complete thought. May contain phrases but does not contain additional clauses. May have compound subjects and predicates.

Compound Sentence – Two independent clauses joined by a coordinating conjunction.

Complex Sentence – Contains at least one independent and one dependent clause introduced by a subordinating conjunction.

Compound/Complex Sentence – One compound sentence plus a dependent clause.

Coordinating Conjunction – Joins two independent clauses that could each stand alone as a sentence. The conjunction must be a FANBOY (for, and, nor, but, or, yet, so)

Subordinating Conjunction – Introduces a dependent clause (words like *because, when*).

Preposition – A word that expresses the relationship between two different elements (*The cat sat on the table, She did her homework after dinner*).

Prepositional Phrase – The preposition and what comes directly after it (*on the table, after dinner*).

Adverbial Clause – A dependent clause that acts like an adverb and provides information about the what, where, when, why, how of a verb, adjective, or adverb.

Clause of Reason – Introduced by words like *because, since, and so*, these clauses explain why things happen.

Tips for Using Conjunctions

COORDINATING CONJUNCTIONS

1. *CO* means *with* or *together*.
2. *ORDINATE* means *arranged or ordered*.
3. Coordinating conjunctions join two independent clauses that could each stand alone as sentences.
4. Each side of the sentence contains both a subject and a predicate. Both sides are equal in weight and importance. **They can usually be flipped but may or may not maintain the same meaning.**
5. The result is a COMPOUND SENTENCE.
6. A coordinating conjunction must stay in the middle of the sentence to maintain balance.
7. A comma comes directly before the coordinating conjunction, but only if both sides can be complete sentences.
8. FANBOYS are the only coordinating conjunctions.

SUBORDINATING CONJUNCTIONS

1. *SUB* means *lower, under, dependent*, or *inferior*.
2. *ORDINATE* means *arranged* or *ordered*.
3. Subordinating conjunctions introduce a dependent clause. It depends on an independent clause to make sense.
4. The two sides of the sentence are NOT equal in importance. There is no comma between them when the dependent clause comes last.
5. The result is a COMPLEX SENTENCE.
6. A subordinating conjunction can be moved to the beginning of a sentence, but it must be moved with its clause. They function as a unit.
7. When a sentence is flipped (the dependent clause comes first), there is a comma after the dependent clause.
8. There are many different subordinating conjunctions.

The late William Van Cleave often spoke on the topic of sentence grammar. In his book *Writing Matters*, he came up with a type of shorthand to show how commas work with clauses.

I = Independent Clause
D = Dependent Clause

I, FANBOYS I
I D
D, I

Coordinating Conjunctions
Tip Sheet Graphic

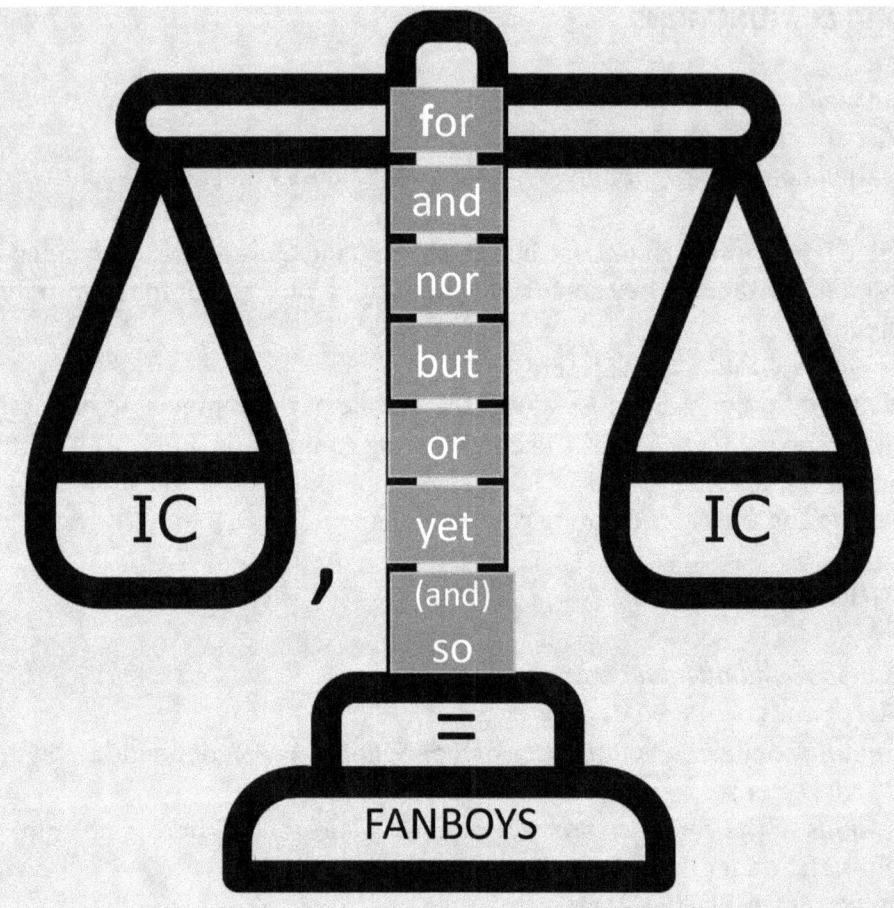

Ex. The boy liked the snacks at the inn, but he did not like the animals.
    The boy did not like the animals, but he did like the snacks at the inn.
    (The meaning changes, but the structure of the sentence is balanced.
     Both sides are equal.)

Ex. He will stay at the inn, or he will go back to class.
    He will go back to class, or he will stay at the inn.

Note: Because both sides are equal, the coordinating conjunction must stay
in the middle to maintain balance.

Subordinating Conjunctions
Tip Sheet Graphic

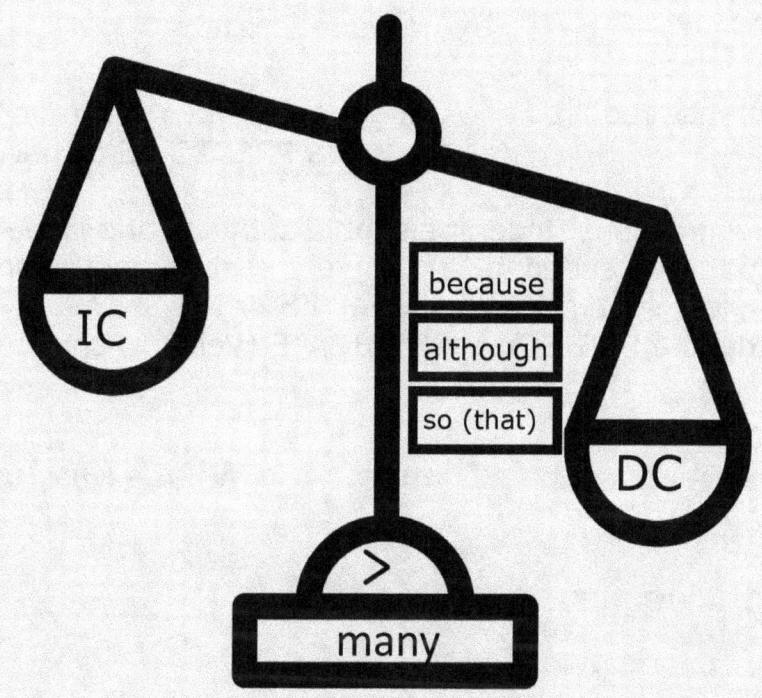

Ex. The boy skipped class because he was tired of taking tests.

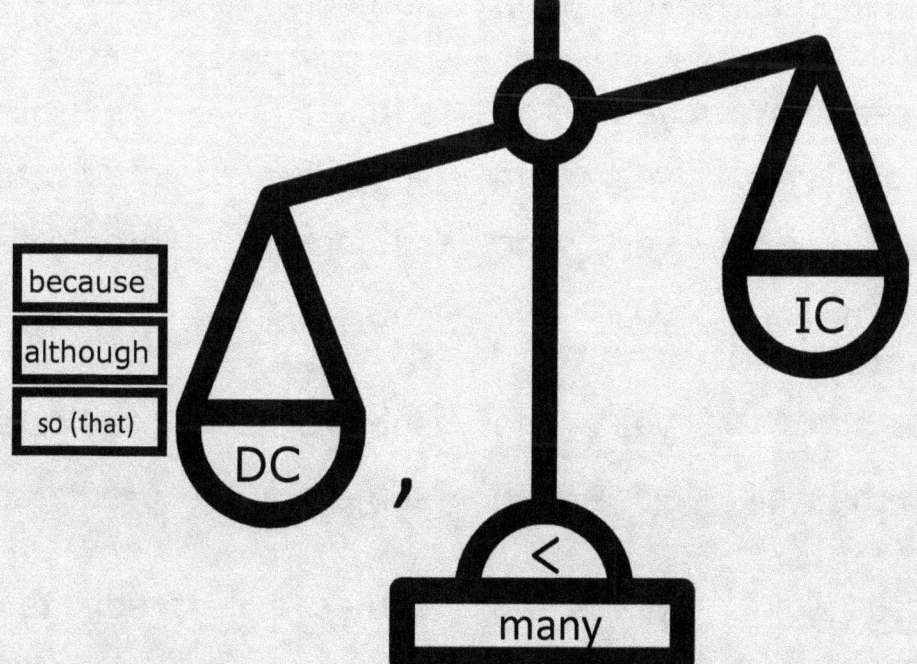

Ex. Because the boy was tired of taking tests, he skipped class.

Note: Because both sides are NOT equal, the subordinating conjunction can be in the middle or beginning of the sentence.

Sentence Construction #1
Identifying Complete Sentences
based on *The Raven Remix*
by Carolee Dean

A complete sentence requires two things: a SUBJECT (Who or What is the Doer)
+ a PREDICATE (What they are Doing)

Directions:
1. Read each line below. Underline simple subjects and circle simple predicates (verbs). Both are needed for a complete sentence, but some are missing.
2. Is it a complete sentence? underline YES or NO.
3. If NO - underline SUBJECT or PREDICATE (Verb) to show what is missing.

Line of Verse	Complete		What's Missing?	
Example (Standing) on a wooden sill.	yes	<u>no</u>	<u>subject</u>	predicate
1. Ed ran in.	yes	no	subject	predicate
2. Shook my hand and greeted me.	yes	no	subject	predicate
3. Cats are upsetting.	yes	no	subject	predicate
4. A cat of evil ped·ĭ·gree.	yes	no	subject	predicate
5. Kitten.	yes	no	subject	predicate
6. He grabbed the beets and greens.	yes	no	subject	predicate
7. I felt a rapping.	yes	no	subject	predicate
8. Tapping on the wall by me.	yes	no	subject	predicate
9. Two black sockets.	yes	no	subject	predicate
10. Creeping from an open pit.	yes	no	subject	predicate

ANSWERS

Line of Verse	Complete		What's Missing?	
1. Ed (ran) in.	<u>yes</u>	no	subject	predicate
2. (Shook) my hand and (greeted) me.	yes	<u>no</u>	<u>subject</u>	predicate
3. Cats (are) upsetting.	<u>yes</u>	no	subject	predicate
4. A <u>cat</u> of evil ped·ĭ·gree.	yes	<u>no</u>	subject	<u>predicate</u>
5. <u>Kitten</u>.	yes	<u>no</u>	subject	<u>predicate</u>
6. He (grabbed) the beets and greens.	<u>yes</u>	no	subject	predicate
7. I (felt) a rapping.	<u>yes</u>	no	subject	predicate
8. (Tapping) on the wall by me.	yes	<u>no</u>	<u>subject</u>	predicate
9. Two black <u>sockets</u>.	yes	<u>no</u>	subject	<u>predicate</u>
10. (Creeping) from an open pit.	yes	<u>no</u>	<u>subject</u>	predicate

Sentence Construction #2
Compound Subjects & Predicates
based on *The Raven Remix*
by Carolee Dean

A simple sentence can have a compound subject or a compound verb/predicate. Underline subjects and circle predicates. Then underline the correct description below it.

Examples:
The <u>boy</u> (ate) muffins and chicken.   none
The <u>boy</u> (ate) and (drank).   compound predicate
The <u>boy</u> and the <u>man</u> (ate)   compound subject

The raven crept across the mantel.

compound subject   compound predicate   none

Ed cooked and served the crusted shrimp.

compound subject   compound predicate   none

The bug fell and crashed onto the floor.

compound subject   compound predicate   none

Some script was printed in the middle of the riddle.

compound subject   compound predicate   none

Ed and the boy looked for the chest of trinkets and cash.

compound subject   compound predicate   none

The mammal grinned and went into the kitchen.

compound subject   compound predicate   none

The cats hissed and scratched.

compound subject   compound predicate   none

The kid dropped the brass rings and the crimson vest.

compound subject   compound predicate   none

196

ANSWERS

The raven crept across the mantel.

compound subject   compound predicate   **none**

Ed cooked and served the crusted shrimp.

compound subject   **compound predicate**   none

The bug fell and crashed onto the floor.

compound subject   **compound predicate**   none

Script was printed in the middle of the riddle.

compound subject   compound predicate   **none**

Ed and the boy looked for the chest of trinkets and cash.

compound subject   compound predicate   none

The mammal grinned and went into the kitchen.

compound subject   **compound predicate**   none

The cats hissed and scratched.

compound subject   **compound predicate**   none

The kid dropped the brass rings and the crimson vest.

compound subject   compound predicate   none

Sentence Construction #3
Direct Objects
based on *The Raven Remix*
by Carolee Dean

Fill in the blanks with a direct objects from the story.

Examples:
The boy opened <u>the book</u>.
He ate <u>chicken legs and waffles</u>.

1. The boy skipped _____.

2. Ed cooked _____.

3. The bug stung _____.

4. The boy smashed _____.

5. Ed sold _____ at the inn.

6. Ed and the boy solved _____.

7. They opened _____.

8. They stuffed _____ in their pockets.

9. The cat scratched _____.

10. The o-rang o-tang slung _____.

ANSWERS MAY VARY

1. The boy skipped <u>class</u>.

2. Ed cooked <u>chicken, snacks, muffins etc…</u>.

3. The bug stung <u>the boy</u>.

4. The boy smashed <u>the bug</u>.

5. Ed sold <u>pets, snacks, books etc…</u> at the inn.

6. Ed and the boy solved <u>the puzzle, the riddle, the code…</u>.

7. They opened <u>the chest</u>.

8. They stuffed <u>trinkets, rings, jewels, etc…</u>in their pockets.

9. The cat scratched <u>the table</u>.

10. The o-rang o-tang slung <u>food and trash</u>.

Sentence Construction #4
Sentence Combining
based on *The Raven Remix*
by Carolee Dean

Directions:
Use the conjunction in **bold** to combine 2 short sentences into one sentence.

Example:
(and) The dog can run. The dog can bark.
The dog can run, and it can bark.   OR
The dog can run and bark.

(and) Ed gave him shrimp. Ed gave him muffins.

(but) The boy said he was going back to class. It was well past three.

(or) Will the boy stay? Will the boy go?

(nor) The boy did not like the cat. The boy did not like the o-rang o-tang.

(so) Ravens started hatching. The boy ran.

(yet) The boy should have been in class. The boy went to the inn.

(for) The boy needed a rest. The boy had been taking tests.

Sentence Construction #4
Sentence Combining
based on *The Raven Remix*
by Carolee Dean

ANSWERS.

(and) Ed gave him shrimp. Ed gave him muffins.
Ed gave him shrimp, and he gave him muffins. OR
Ed gave him shrimp and muffins.

(but) The boy said he was going back to class. It was well past three.
The boy said he was going back to class, but it was well past three.

(or) Will the boy stay? Will the boy go?
Will the boy stay, or will he go? OR
Will the boy stay or go?

(nor) The boy did not like the cat. The boy did not like the o-rang o-tang. **The boy did not like the cat, nor did he like the o-rang o-tang**. OR **The boy did not like the cat nor the o-rang o-tang.**

(so) Ravens started hatching. The boy ran.
Ravens started hatching, so the boy ran.

(yet) The boy should have been in class. The boy went to the inn.
The boy should have been in class, yet he went to the inn.

(for) The boy needed a rest. The boy had been testing.
The boy needed a rest, for he had been testing.

Sentence Construction #5
Clauses and Phrases
based on *The Raven Remix*
by Carolee Dean

Phrases and clauses are groups of words that act as a unit. The difference is that a clause contains both a subject and a predicate.

1. For each item below, start by circling the predicate (verb).
2. If there is a predicate, underline the subject if there is one.
    (Note: Prepositional phrases will not have a subject nor a predicate).
3. If there is both a subject and a predicate, write <u>Clause</u> on the line. If not, write <u>Phrase</u>.

Example:
because the <u>mammal</u> (was swinging)   Clause
on the kettle   Phrase

1. in the apple strudel _____

2. when Ed set pickles on the table _____

3. next to the kettle and the ladle _____

4. the beetle fell in the middle of the sheet _____

5. on the simple ample wooden chest _____

6. after he ate the maple waffle _____

7. the riddle was a jumble of ABCs _____

8. was it a little needle _____

9. he solved the final puzzle _____

10. with a fumble and a bumble _____

Note: Nouns that appear in prepositional phrases are not the subject of the clause.

ANSWERS

1. in the apple strudel   <u>Phrase</u>

2. when <u>Ed</u> (set) pickles on the table   <u>Clause</u>

3. next to the kettle and the ladle   <u>Phrase</u>

4. the <u>beetle</u> (fell) in the middle of the sheet   <u>Clause</u>

5. on the simple ample wooden chest   <u>Phrase</u>

6. after <u>he</u> (ate) the maple waffle   <u>Clause</u>

7. the <u>riddle</u> (was) a jumble of ABCs   <u>Clause</u>

8. (was) <u>it</u> a little needle?   <u>Clause</u>

9. <u>he</u> (solved) the final puzzle   <u>Clause</u>

10. with a fumble and a bumble   <u>Phrase</u>

Sentence Construction #6
Independent and Dependent Clauses
based on *The Raven Remix*
by Carolee Dean

Clauses can be Independent (I) and stand alone as complete sentences or Dependent (D). Dependent clauses need to be paired with an Independent Clause to make sense. Write I or D next to the clauses below to indicate if they are Dependent or Independent.

Example:
the stunning raven was standing on the mantel   <u>I</u>
because the skillet was hot   <u>D</u>

1. he snacked on spiral ham _____

2. when Ed set strudel on the table _____

3. he was swinging and slinging hash _____

4. the script looked like a scramble of ABCs _____

5. after the student skipped math class _____

6. the chest was filled with splendid trinkets and vests _____

7. since it was stocked with stuff _____

8. because the bug stung him _____

9. the inn sat silent and still _____

10. when he sprinted from the inn _____

ANSWERS

1. he snacked on spiral ham I

2. when Ed set strudel on the table D

3. it was swinging and slinging hash I

4. the script looked like a scramble of ABCs I

5. after the student skipped math class D

6. the chest was filled with splendid trinkets and vests I

7. since it was stocked with stuff D

8. because the bug stung him D

9. the inn sat silent and still I

10. when he sprinted from the inn D

Note: With a capital and a period, an independent clause would also be a sentence.

Sentence Construction #7
Where Things Happen
based on *The Raven Remix*
by Carolee Dean

EXAMPLE:
1. Read the sentences below.
2. Underline the part of the sentence that tells WHERE the action is happening.

Example: The inn sat <u>on a vacant hill</u>.

1. The raven stood on the mantel.

2. Cap'n Kidd hid the cash in the chest.

3. Richmond is in the state of Virginia.

4. The bug stung the kid on the cheek.

5. The map fell next to the bug.

Create your own sentence below. Include a subject, predicate, and location.

_____

_____

ANSWERS

1. The raven stood <u>on the mantel</u>.

2. Cap'n Kidd hid the cash <u>in the chest</u>.

3. Richmond is <u>in the state of Virginia</u>.

4. The bug stung the kid <u>on the cheek</u>.

5. The map fell <u>next to the bug</u>.

Sentence Construction #8
Sentence Flip for "Where"
based on *The Raven Remix*
by Carolee Dean

1. Read the sentences below.
2. Underline the part of the sentence that tells the location WHERE the action is happening.
3. In some sentences, the location is flipped, and it comes first. When that happens, the location is followed by a comma. Put a star next to these sentences. ★

Example: Cats were scratching <u>on the table</u>.

Flipped: <u>On the table</u>, cats were scratching.★

1. By my foot, I felt a thumping.

2. On my skin, I felt a clinging.

3. From the jacket of a book, the cunning raven peered at me.

4. On a wooden sill, a stunning raven looked at me.

5. It crashed and landed with a tweet on a fragment by my feet.

Create your own sentence on the back of this page. Include a subject, predicate, and location. When you are done, write the sentence again, but this time flip it to make the location come first.

ANSWERS

1. <u>By my foot</u>, I felt a thumping.

2. <u>On my skin</u>, I felt a clinging.

3. <u>From the jacket of a book</u>, the cunning raven peered at me.

4. <u>On a wooden sill</u>, a stunning raven looked at me.

5. It crashed and landed with a tweet <u>on a fragment by my feet</u>.

Sentence Construction #9
When Things Happen
based on *The Raven Remix*
by Carolee Dean

1. Read the sentences below.
2. Underline the part of the sentence that gives information about the time or WHEN the action is happening.

Example: The ruckus in the kitchen stopped <u>when he left the inn</u>.

1. Don't skip class next week.

2. The cat jumped on the table as I opened the book.

3. He said he had to go at three o'clock.

4. I felt a bug sting me as I sat.

5. The beetle beeped when it fell.

Create your own sentence below. Include a subject, predicate, and time information.

_____

_____

_____

Sentence Construction #9
When Things Happen
based on *The Raven Remix*
by Carolee Dean

ANSWERS

1. Don't skip class <u>next week</u>.

2. The cat jumped on the table <u>as I opened the book</u>.

3. He said he had to go <u>at three o'clock</u>.

4. I felt a bug sting me <u>as I sat</u>.

5. The beetle beeped <u>when it fell</u>.

Sentence Construction #10
Sentence Flip for "When"
based on *The Raven Remix*
by Carolee Dean

1. Read the sentences.
2. Underline the part that tells WHEN the action is happening.
3. In some sentences, the time frame is flipped and comes first. If that happens, the "when" information is followed by a comma. Draw a star next to these sentences. ✦

Example: The ruckus in the kitchen stopped <u>when he left the inn</u>.

Flipped: <u>When he left the inn</u>, the ruckus in the kitchen stopped. ✦

---

1. Next week, don't skip class.

2. As I opened the book, the cat jumped on the table.

3. He said he had to go at three o'clock.

4. As I sat, I felt a bug sting me.

5. When it fell, the beetle beeped.

Create your own sentence on the back of this page. Include a subject, predicate, and time frame. When you are done, write the sentence again, but flip it to make the time frame come first.

ANSWERS

1. <u>Next week</u>, don't skip class. ✸

2. <u>As I opened the book,</u> the cat jumped on the table. ✸

3. He said he had to go <u>at three o'clock</u>.

4. <u>As I sat</u>, I felt the bug sting me. ✸

5. <u>When it fell</u>, the beetle beeped. ✸

If students are confused that sentence #1 does not seem to have a subject, you may explain that for an imperative sentence (a sentence that gives a direct command) the implied subject is YOU.

Sentence Construction #11
Why Things Happen
A Clause with a Cause
based on *The Raven Remix* by Carolee Dean

The subordinating conjunctions **because** and **since** can introduce what is called a "clause of reason." These dependent clauses explain the causes of events in the main or independent clause.

1. Look at subordinating conjunctions below in bold.
2. Read the story and then finish the sentences below giving a reason for the event that happens in the main clause.

Example: The boy went to the inn **because** he was avoiding class.
The boy decided to stay **since** Ed offered him free snacks.

1. The boy opened the book **since**

2. The boy smashed the bug **because**

3. Ed and the boy went looking for treasure **because**

4. The boy dropped the trinkets **because**

5. Ed gave the boy the note **because**

Sentence Construction #11
Why Things Happen

ANSWERS MAY VARY

1. The boy opened the book **since** <u>the raven told him to peek inside</u>.

2. The boy smashed the bug **because** <u>it stung him</u>.

3. Ed and the boy went looking for treasure **because** <u>the secret code said riches were hidden at the inn.</u>

4. The boy dropped the trinkets **because** <u>the room filled with alarming animals.</u>

5. Ed gave the boy the note **because** <u>he wanted him to stay in class next week.</u>

Sentence Construction #12
Sentence Flips for "Why"
based on *The Raven Remix* by Carolee Dean

1. Look at the sentences below.
2. Flip each sentence by rewriting it and putting the "Why" clause first.
3. Remember to put a comma after the "why" clause.
4. Use another piece of paper if you run out of room.

Example: The boy went to the inn **because** he was avoiding class.

Flipped: Because he was avoiding class, the boy went to the inn.

1. The boy opened the book **since** the raven told him to peek inside.

2. The boy smashed the bug **because** it stung him.

3. Ed and the boy went looking for treasure **because** the secret code said riches were hidden at the inn.

4. The boy dropped the trinkets **because** the room filled with alarming animals.

5. Ed gave the boy the note **because** he wanted him to stay in class next week.

Write a sentence about the story on the back of this page and start your sentence with **because**.

ANSWERS

.

1. The boy opened the book **since** the raven told him to peek inside.
Since the raven told him to peek inside, the boy opened the book.

2. The boy smashed the bug **because** it stung him.
Because it stung him, the boy smashed the bug.

3. Ed and the boy went looking for treasure **because** the secret code said riches were hidden at the inn.
Because the secret code said riches were hidden at the inn, Ed and the boy went looking for treasure.

4. The boy dropped the trinkets **because** the room filled with alarming animals.
Because the room filled with alarming animals, the boy dropped the trinkets.

5. Ed gave the boy the note **because** he wanted him to stay in class the next week.

Because he wanted him to stay in class the next week, Ed gave the boy the note.

Sentence Construction #13
Who is Doing What?
based on *The Raven Remix*
by Carolee Dean

Directions:
1. Pick an illustration from the book.
2. Describe what is going on in the illustration by answering the questions below.
3. Use your answers to construct one long complex sentence.

Question		Response
1. **Who** is the main character in the illustration?		
2. **Which** character (scared, happy, tall)		
3. **What** are they doing?		
4. **How** are they doing it? (ex. quickly, slowly, backward)		
5. **Where** is it happening?		
6. **When** is it happening?		
5. **Why** are they doing it? This may not be in the picture.		

Use the information above to create one long sentence. Write it on a separate piece of paper.

Sentence Construction #14
Sentence Quest Images
(*Specter*)
based on *The Raven Remix*
by Carolee Dean

Directions: Use one of the images below and answer the Sentence Quest Questions on the next page. **Bonus:** Use the word ***specter*** and at least one other ***spect*** word from the word matrix below in your sentence. You may refer back to the words you created for the **spect** activity in the morphology section. A specter is something that is seen as an apparition, image, phantom, or ghost.

Graveyard Ghost

Skeleton Band

Raven in the Woods

Scarecrow Pumpkin

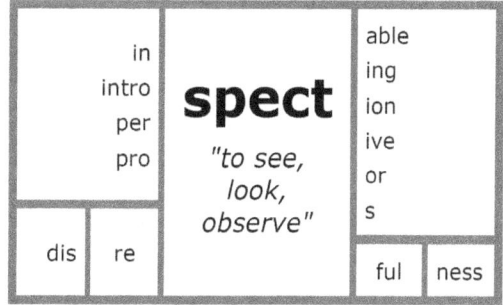

	in		able
	intro	**spect**	ing
	per		ion
	pro	*"to see, look, observe"*	ive
			or
			s
dis	re		ful	ness

Created with *Mini Matrix-Maker*, at www.neilramsden.co.uk/spelling/matrix

Sentence Construction #14
Sentence Quest Questions
based on *The Raven Remix*
by Carolee Dean

Directions: Paste an image here from the previous page or draw one of your own. Then, answer the questions below. Use the blank *Sentence Quest* page and try to fit all of the information below into one long sentence. **Bonus:** Use the word ***specter*** and at least one other ***spect*** word in your sentence.

A **specter** is something that is seen as an apparition, image, phantom, or ghost.

Who or What is the subject of your sentence?

_____

Which one? (Describe the subject- tall, thin, red...)

_____

What are they doing?

_____

How are they doing it?_____

Where?_____

When?_____

Why?_____

_____

Sentence Construction #14
Sentence Quest – Blank Page
based on *The Raven Remix*
by Carolee Dean

Directions:
1. Use the answers from *Sentence Quest Questions* to create one long sentence below. Try to use the word **specter** and at least one other **spect** word in your sentence. Your sentence can be funny, silly, or scary.
2. Use your sentence as the start of a story.

_____

_____

_____

_____

_____

_____

_____

_____

_____

_____

_____

Sentence Construction #15
Just for Fun
Hiding Whodunnit

based on *The Raven Remix*
by Carolee Dean

Directions: Take the simple sentence below from the story of "The Purloined Letter" and try to confuse amateur sleuth Dupin by hiding the identity of the guilty party among as many additional clauses and phrases as you can create. Note: This is just for fun. It is NOT a good way to write when we want our communication to be clear and to the point. As a bonus, can you add extra characters to the mix?

Mr. D. stole the letter.

_____

_____

_____

_____

_____

_____

_____

_____

_____

_____

_____

_____

STORY FRAMES

INTRODUCTION

The Story Analysis in this section is based on my book, *Story Frames for Teaching Literacy: Enhancing Student Learning Through the Power of Storytelling* (Paul H. Brookes Publishing Co., 2021). That book is not needed to complete this story analysis on the next few pages, but if you would like to take a deeper dive into narrative intervention with access to 35 adaptable lesson plans along with downloadable resources, you can find my book at Brookes Publishing. The lesson plans include a more detailed approach to summary writing as well as a detailed discussion of how writing expectations change across the grade levels.

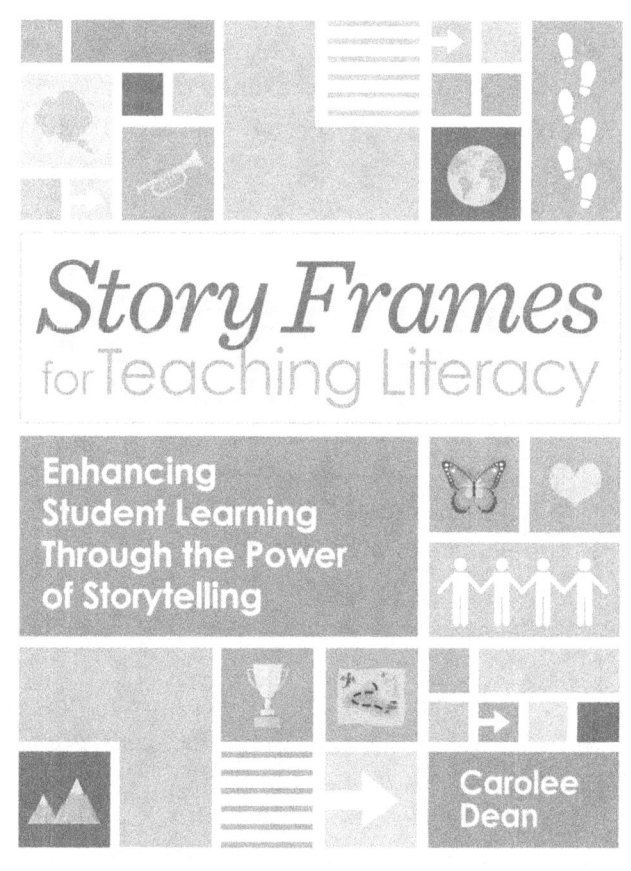

STORY FRAMES

PLOT ANALYSIS

The BASIC STORYBOARD is based upon the traditional story analysis outlined by Stein, N., & Glenn, C. (1979). An analysis of story comprehension in elementary school children. In R. Freedle (Ed.), New directions in discourse processing (Vol. 2, pp. 53-120). Norwood, NJ: Ablex.

Their story elements include *setting, initiating events, internal responses, internal plans, attempts, direct consequences*, and *reactions*. The 8 elements of the *Story Frames* BASIC STORYBOARD are below:

1. **Ordinary World**: The Main Character (MC) and setting are described.
2. **Call and Response**: An initiating event occurs to get the action going and the main character's inward and/or outward response to that event are described.
3. **Problems and Prizes:** A problem or a prize (or both) are described
4. **Plans**: The MC makes plans that may be obvious or implied.
5. **Attempt**: The MC attempts to attain the goal with consequences.
6. **Attempt**: The MC makes another attempt to attain the goal with consequences.
7. **Climax**: A final attempt to attain the goal is made.
8. **Reward**: The MC receives an award or consequence. Internal responses to the events and outcome of the story are explored.

The BASIC STORYBOARD is from *Story Frames for Teaching Literacy: Enhancing Student Learning Through the Power of Storytelling* (Brookes Publishing, 2021) by Carolee Dean

1. After reading the story poem, the student uses the blank version of the BASIC STORYBOARD and either draws stick figures, writes keywords, or both in each square to show what is happening in each frame of the story. Model as needed. This step may be completed as a class or individually. Storyboards with the content described are for teacher reference.
2. Have students brainstorm a list of keywords to write in the vocabulary section of the storyboard.
3. The completed student storyboard may then be used to retell the story verbally or to write a summary. Each row of the storyboard creates a paragraph, except for the bottom row, which functions like a word wall and contains key terms.
4. An 8x11 printable version of each storyboard may be found in the downloadable PDFs. Find the code near the end of this Activity Book.

The longer, COMPLETE STORYBOARD version with 12 story frames is available on page 133 of Story Frames for Teaching Literacy: Enhancing Student Learning Through the Power of Storytelling.

STORY FRAMES

PLOT ANALYSIS

Story Frames (Basic Version) – THE RAVEN REMIX by Carolee Dean			
Ordinary World	**Call & Response**	**Problem & Prize**	**Plan**
Attempt	**Attempt**	**Climax**	**Reward**

Vocabulary	**People & Places**	**Conjunctions**		**Transitions**
	kid	and	although	first
	Ed A. P.	but	before	eventually
	raven	yet	after	next
	black cat	or	unless	consequently
	gold bug	so	while	last
	O-rang o-tang	then	where	surprisingly
	school	because	even if	in addition
	Ed A. P. Book Stop, Pet	when		finally
	Shop, Inn & Grill			as a result

STORY FRAMES

Story Frames for Teaching Literacy

Enhancing Student Learning Through the Power of Storytelling

Carolee Dean

PLOT ANALYSIS

Story Frames (Basic Version) – THE RAVEN REMIX by Carolee Dean

Ordinary World	Call & Response	Problem & Prize	Plan
A boy skips class and visits the Ed A.P. Book Stop, Pet Shop, Inn and Grill.	A raven tells him to look inside a book. The boy opens it, and it starts to bend and twist. Animals come out.	A black cat scares the young man, but Ed convinces him to stay and have a snack. They discover a code that tells them there is a treasure chest hidden at the inn.	They set off on a quest to find the treasure by searching the inn. (Implied plan)

Attempt or Event	Attempt or Event	Climax	Reward
Ed and the boy go room to room looking for the treasure, but they don't find anything.	Ed and the boy finally go back to the kitchen where they started. They realize that what they thought was a bench is actually the treasure chest.	They find many valuable things in the chest, but animals start a ruckus and cause the boy to drop the trinkets.	He runs to his jeep. Ed gives him one last bonus tip --to stay in class next week.

Vocabulary	Characters & Places	Conjunctions		Transitions
	Kid Ed A. P. raven black cat gold bug O-rang o-tang School Ed A. P. Book Stop, Pet Shop, Inn & Grill	and but yet or so then because when	although before after unless while where even if	first eventually next consequently last surprisingly in addition finally as a result

COMPREHENSION

INTRODUCTION

PAGES – The PAGES strategy includes five key elements that have been shown to improve comprehension. They may be used while listening or reading. **P=** Pause and Picture, **A=** Ask Questions, **G =** Go Back or Go Forward, **E =** Explore Words and Sentences, **S =** Summarize

What's Your Text Type? –Knowing text types helps the reader frame the information and understand the author's purpose. In this activity, students first learn about the features of the different types of text in the Text Types Guide and some signal words that go with each type. Then, they read an excerpt based on *The Raven Remix* and use the Text Type Guide to help them decide on the text type.

Comprehension Questions - Many older students are expected to answer questions using a RACE format or something similar. Struggling learners need this process broken down into manageable steps and modeled. After reading or listening to the summary of "The God Bug" in *The Raven Remix* chapter book, students answer comprehension questions by restating the question before providing the answer. Word count and approximate grade level are provided in the chapter book if you would like to calculate reading fluency either before or after reading for comprehension. Headings are not included in the word count. Remember that many students with writing challenges will need the additional support of being able to answer verbally or use a voice-to-text option to create written responses. That's okay. They are still learning the grade level expectations and are growing in their ability to give more detailed answers.

RACE Responses - Students ready for complete RACE Responses may add to their responses above by citing evidence from the text and further explaining their answers. Students with learning differences may need the selection read aloud for them a second or third time.

Struggling readers often miss out on these rich writing opportunities. Even after their decoding skills improve, they may still lag behind their peers in written language development. It is important to scaffold these advanced written responses and provide adequate support so that written language goals are both challenging and attainable.

Dean, C. (2021). *Story frames for teaching literacy: Enhancing student learning through the power of storytelling*. Baltimore, MD: Paul H. Brookes Publishing Co.

Hennessy, N.L. (2021). *The reading comprehension blueprint: Helping students make meaning from text*. Baltimore, MD: Paul H. Brookes Publishing Co.

PAGES

From *The Raven Remix Activity Book*
By Carolee Dean

Use this strategy when reading or listening to something read aloud.

Picture – Pause after a **period**, a **paragraph**, or a **page** of text and try to form a mental **picture** of what you have just read.

Ask – There are many questions you might **ask** yourself about what you have read, but the first and most important two are, "Was I able to form a picture?" and "Does that picture make sense?" You may also **ask** clarification questions and questions about Who is Doing What? Also, **ask** yourself if there are words that you don't know or that don't make sense.

Go Back or Go Forward – Do you need to **go back** and reread what you just read? Sometimes, you need to keep moving **forward**. A confusing word or reference may become clearer in the next sentence or when you finish the sentence you are reading.

Explore Words and Sentences- Are there unfamiliar **words** or concepts that need to be looked up in the dictionary or in another reference? Do you need to read the sentence more carefully to figure out who is doing what?

Summarize – Once the above steps have been taken, put the information into your own words. If you are not ready to **summarize**, you may need to go back and explore some of the steps again.

Text Type Guide

From *The Raven Remix Activity Book*
By Carolee Dean

Use the information below to decide on the text types in the next activity.

Type of Text	Signal Words
Description – Sensory details are used to describe a person, place, or thing.	looks like, sounds like, feels like, for example, such as, characterized by
Sequence – an order of events, timeline, or steps in a process.	before, during, after, first, second, next, then, finally
Compare and Contrast – How two or more things are alike or different.	same, as well as, similar, in common, different, although, however, on the other hand, in comparison, either/or
Problem and Solution – What is wrong and how to fix it.	because, resolved, result, so that, consequently,
Cause and Effect – How or why an event happened and the result.	because, since, as a result, caused by, led to, therefore, when/then, if/then

Dean, C. (2021). *Story frames for teaching literacy: Enhancing student learning through the power of storytelling*. Baltimore, MD: Paul H. Brookes Publishing Co.

Hennessy, N.L. (2021). *The reading comprehension blueprint: Helping students make meaning from text*. Baltimore, MD: Paul H. Brookes Publishing Co.

What's My Text Type? (1-3)

Directions: Read each paragraph below from *The Raven Remix* by Carolee Dean. Identify which paragraph goes with which text type.

1. A parody usually focuses on exaggerating a specific literary work. *The Raven Remix* does this by following the same rhyme and meter pattern as Poe's classic tale of "The Raven." A raven is central to both stories. In contrast, the *Remix* is humorous, while "The Raven" is quite serious. Another difference is that *The Raven Remix* references several characters or objects found in other tales by Edgar Allan Poe. It is still considered a parody because the focus is on the work of one author.

2. In the story "The Pit and the Pendulum," a man wakes up in a cold, dark room. He hears mice crawling out of a pit and smells food nearby. He can't see anything, so he explores the room by touching the rough stone walls.

3. The police ask Dupin for help because they cannot find the stolen letter. Dupin studies Minister D. and concludes that he would have hidden the letter in plain sight. He visits the man's home so that he can look for the letter, which he sees in a rack of cards. Dupin observes that it has been disguised to look like a letter from someone else. Dupin notes its appearance, goes home, and creates a duplicate because he wants to swap the letters. The next time he visits Minister D., Dupin gets the stolen letter. Consequently, he is able to give the stolen letter to the police.

Test Type:	Paragraph #:
Description	_____
Sequence	_____
Compare and Contrast	_____
Problem and Solution	_____
Cause and Effect	_____

What's My Text Type? (4-6)

Directions: Read each paragraph below from *The Raven Remix* by Carolee Dean. Identify which paragraph goes with which text type.

4. On September 24, 1849, three days before leaving for New York, Poe gave a lecture and poetry reading. His sister, Rose, and Elmira Shelton were both present. On Wednesday, September 26, Poe met with his friend, Thompson, who later said that Poe was in a cheerful mood and seemed to be looking forward to the future. By that evening, his mood had changed.

5. Poe's death certificate listed phrenitis (swelling of the brain) as the cause of his death. Some people think that because he had a fever, Poe may have been suffering from flu that led to pneumonia after his exposure to the storm that occurred the day before he was found in the pub. A high fever can result in swelling of the brain with symptoms of hallucination and confusion.

6. Tuberculosis was also called "consumption" because a person with the disease seemed to be consumed as they lost weight and wasted away. They looked thin and pale, but their cheeks were often rosy because of a low-grade fever. Blood often came out of their mouth as they coughed. They were frequently tired and might stay in bed all day as the disease progressed.

Test Type: **Paragraph #:**
Description   _____
Sequence   _____
Compare and Contrast   _____
Problem and Solution   _____
Cause and Effect   _____

What's My Text Type?

ANSWERS

Paragraphs 1-3

Test Type:	**Paragraph #:**
Description	___2___
Sequence	_____
Compare and Contrast	___1___
Problem and Solution	___3___
Cause and Effect	_____

Paragraphs 4-6

Test Type:	**Paragraph #:**
Description	___6___
Sequence	___4___
Compare and Contrast	_____
Problem and Solution	_____
Cause and Effect	___5___

Comprehension Questions about
"The Gold Bug"

Directions:

1. READ or LISTEN to the summary of "The Gold Bug" from pages 58-59 of *The Raven Remix: A Mashup of Poe Titles by Carolee Dean*.

2. RESTATE the questions below on a separate piece of paper.

3. ANSWER the question in your own words in a complete sentence. Leave several blank lines between answers. You may need to come back later to add more information.

EXAMPLE

QUESTION: What two things does William Legrand find?

ANSWER: (answers will vary) William Legrand finds a gold bug and a piece of vellum near it.

Questions:

1. What is vellum?

2. What does the narrator see on the vellum?

3. How does LeGrand figure out what is written on the vellum?

4. Why is the message on the vellum important to the story?

Answers

for Comprehension Questions

Make sure students have restated the question and answered it in a complete sentence. Answers may vary.

1. What is vellum?

Vellum is calfskin.

2. What does the narrator see on the vellum?
The narrator sees strange marks (or... a secret message) on the vellum.

3. How does LeGrand figure out what is written on the vellum?
LeGrand figures out what is written on the vellum by using cryptography.

4. Why is the message on the vellum important to the story?
The message on the vellum is important to the story because it leads Legrand and the narrator to a treasure.

RACE Responses for "The Gold Bug"

Directions: Go back to your answers for the Comprehension Questions. Choose one of them and write a complete RACE response. You should have already completed **R** and **A** in the previous activity. Now add **C** and **E**. **Cite** the evidence and **Explain (or Expand)**.

R – Restate the question

A– Answer the question

C – Cite the evidence from the text to support your answer.

E – Explain (or Expand) your answer

EXAMPLE

QUESTION: What two things does William Legrand find?

ANSWER: (answers will vary) William Legrand finds a gold bug and a piece of vellum near it. **The text states, "The narrator's friend, William Legrand, finds a strange beetle that seems to be covered in gold." Legrand takes these things home, and he shows them to the narrator which results in a search for hidden treasure.**

Possible RACE Responses

Answers may vary. Remind students that the answer, the citation, and the explanation should differ. Some students tend to say the same thing for all three making their response very redundant. You may want to do the first response together to demonstrate.

1. Show students a weak example. Ask them what makes it weak and how it could be improved.
2. Brainstorm synonyms and related terms for keywords. (*writing, script, message, map… hidden, secret, confusing*)
3. Make connections to personal experiences. Ask students what kind of writing people keep for a long time (maps, letters, recipes, birthday cards).
4. Provide writing assistance , such as speech-to- text tools or scribes, for those who need it.

Question #1 – What is Vellum?

Weak Example for #1
Vellum is a calfskin used for writing. The text states, "He finds a piece of vellum, a calfskin used for writing." You can write things on vellum.

Strong Example for #1
Vellum is calfskin. The text states, "Vellum is used to write things you want to keep for a long time." Calfskin lasts longer than paper, so it's useful for things like messages you need to save and maps.

Question #2 - What does the narrator see on the vellum?

Weak Example for #2
The narrator discovers strange marks on the calfskin. The text states, "The narrator discovers strange markings on the calfskin." The markings on the calfskin are strange.

Possible RACE Responses (Continued)

for RACE Responses

Strong Example for #2
The narrator sees confusing writing on the vellum that he doesn't understand. When Legrand returns home, the text states, "He shows the bug and the calfskin to the narrator, who discovers strange markings on the calfskin." The hidden message is a code, and it takes them a while to figure out what it means.

3. How does Legrand figure out what is written on the vellum?

Weak Example for #3
Legrand uses the science of cryptography to figure out what is written on the vellum. The text states, "Legrand uses the science of cryptography to decipher the hidden message." The message is hard to figure out, so Legrand must use the science of cryptography to decipher the hidden message.

Strong Example for #3
LeGrand figures out what is written on the vellum by using cryptography. The text states, "Legrand uses the science of cryptography to decipher the hidden message." Cryptography is like a secret code. People use it to write messages they want to hide from other people.

Possible RACE Responses (Continued)

for RACE Responses

4. Why is the message on the vellum important to the story?

Weak Example for #3
The message is important because it leads them to a treasure hidden on the island. The text states, "The message leads them to a treasure hidden on the island where Legrand lives." They use the message to find the treasure hidden on the island.

Strong Example for #3

The message on the vellum is important to the story because it leads Legrand and the narrator to a treasure that was hidden on the island by a famous pirate. The text states, "Captain Kidd buried the treasure there long ago." The pirate is probably the person who wrote the secret message with directions to find the treasure so that he could locate his hidden stash later. It appears he never came back for it.

Graphic Organizers for Paragraph & Essay Writing

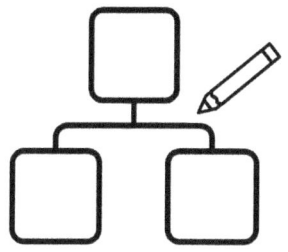

INTRODUCTION

Creature Features – Students look at the book's cover and list the five creatures they find there. They read the decodable story and read or listen to the background information. Then they write down as many details as they can find about each animal, including what Poe story the creature is from.

The following graphic organizers and templates were designed to provide the building blocks needed to create paragraphs and essays. Activities build on each other starting with lists and ending with a multi-paragraph essay. Students benefit from the brainstorming stage, where they talk about how their information could turn into an essay, even if they are not yet ready to write long responses.

1. **Genre Gemstones Brainstorm** – As a group, have students brainstorm characteristics of the various types of stories written by Poe.

2. **Balloon Brainstorm** – Use the Genre Gemstones Brainstorm to compare and contrast gothic fiction and detective stories.

3. **Cause of Death Brainstorm** – More advanced students read the section of *The Raven Remix* that lists the different theories about Poe's death (pages 92-107). They pick the three they think are most plausible and list reasons why those theories make sense.

4. **High Five Writing** – Students incorporate the information from the brainstorms into one or more well-structured paragraphs to be used for a multiple-paragraph essay.

5. **I+P+P+C Multiple Paragraph Essays** - Students follow the directions to incorporate those well-crafted paragraphs from High Five Writing into a multi-paragraph response by simply adding I (Introduction) and C (Conclusion). There are three essays to choose from.

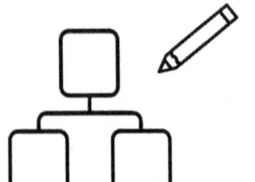

Creature Features
based on *The Raven Remix*
by Carolee Dean

Directions:
1. Look at the cover of *The Raven Remix* and list the five creatures you see.
2. Read the decodable story and the background information.
3. Write down as many details as you can find about each creature, including what story the creature is from.
4. What does the creature do in *The Raven Remix* and the Poe story?

Creature & Story	Description
1. Rat - "The Pit and the Pendulum"	It's a white rodent. In Poe's story, a man rubs food on the ropes tying his hands. Rats chew on the rope, and the man gets free. All it does in *The Raven Remix* is come out of the pit.
2.	
3.	
4.	
5.	

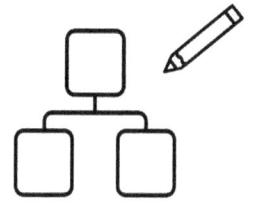

Creature Features
based on *The Raven Remix*
by Carolee Dean

ANSWERS May Vary

Creature & Story	Description
1. Rat "The Pit and the Pendulum"	It's a white rodent. In Poe's story, a man rubs food on the ropes tying his hands. Rats chew on the rope, and the man gets free. All it does in *The Raven Remix* is come out of the pit.
2. Raven "The Raven"	It's a talking blackbird. In Poe's poem, it comes to visit a man at midnight. He asks it questions, and it keeps answering, "Nevermore." In *The Raven Remix* it comes off a book cover and tells a boy to open the book. Weird things come out of the book.
3. Black Cat "The Black Cat"	The cat is black with one eye missing. Its name is Pluto. In Poe's story, it comes back from the dead. In *The Raven Remix* it hisses at the boy and frightens him.
4. Beetle "The Gold Bug"	The beetle is covered in gold and has a black skull on its back. In both stories, it helps lead the narrator to a treasure because of a connection to a piece of secret writing.
5. Orangutan "The Murders in the Rue Morgue"	It's a mammal, like an ape or chimp. In Poe's story, it kills people. In The Raven Remix, it swings from a light, screeches, throws food, and grabs the treasure the boy had found.

GENRE GEMSTONES
Brainstorm
based on *The Raven Remix*
by Carolee Dean

Directions:

Poe is considered by many to be the father of the modern detective story and American gothic fiction. He is also one of the first authors to write science fiction.

1. List the elements that are often included in these genres as discussed in *The Raven Remix.*
2. Name other authors, characters, or works influenced by Poe if any are mentioned.

Genres	Elements	Other Authors/Works
Detective Stories (pages 59-60)		
Gothic Horror (pages 63-64)		
Science Fiction (page 71)		

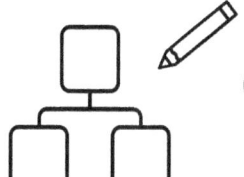

GENRE GEMSTONES
based on *The Raven Remix*
by Carolee Dean

ANSWERS

Genres	Elements	Other Authors/Works
Detective Stories (pages 59-60)	Crime to be solved Murder Amateur Detective C. Auguste Dupin Mystery Deductive reasoning Short story Locked Room Clues in plain sight	Sherlock Holmes Hercule Poirot
Gothic Horror (pages 63-64)	Mystery Horror Death Supernatural elements Romance Gloomy subjects Castles Dungeons Ghosts Country Estates Medieval themes	
Science Fiction (page 71)	Space travel Gadgets Mad scientists Technology Medical experiments	Jules Verne *20,000 Leagues Under the Sea*

Cause of Death
Brainstorm
based on *The Raven Remix*
by Carolee Dean

Directions:
The death of Edgar Allan Poe is a mystery that has never been solved. Read or listen to pages 92-107 of *The Raven Remix* and choose what you think are the top 3 most likely causes of Poe's Death. Explain why that reason makes sense.

Cause of Death	Why it makes sense
Example: Cooping	Cooping was a form of voter fraud where people were kidnapped and forced to vote multiple times wearing disguises. Poe was found at a polling site. He was wearing another man's clothes. He was drunk even though he had taken a vow of temperance.
1.	
2.	
3.	

Balloon Brainstorm
Gothic Horror vs. Detective Stories

from *The Raven Remix* by Carolee Dean

Poe is considered to be the father of the modern detective story as well as the father of American gothic horror.

1. Complete the Genre Gemstones activity.
2. In the middle of the balloon, list the ways gothic fiction and detective stories are similar.
3. On the right and left, list the ways they are different.

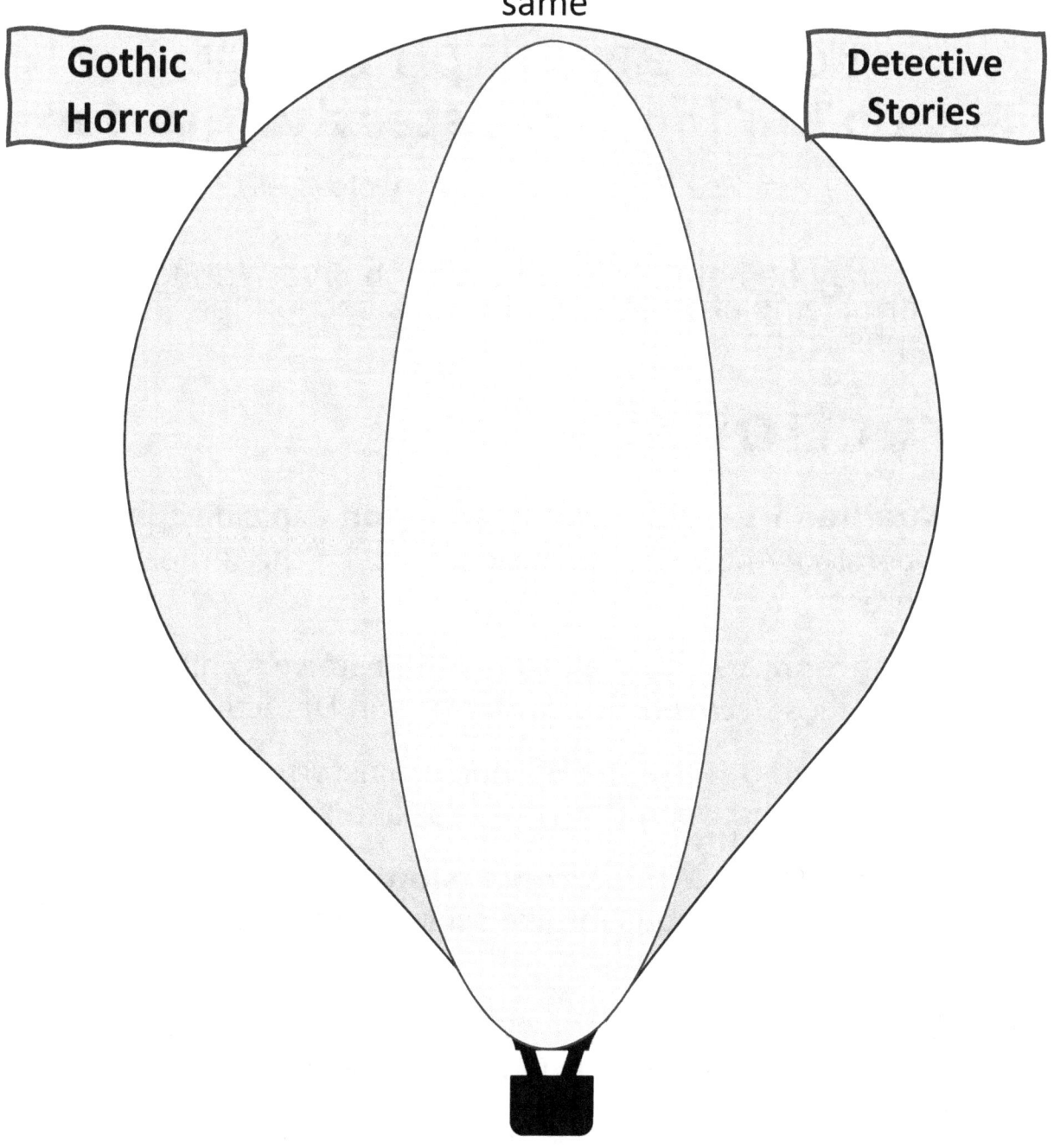

same

Gothic Horror

Detective Stories

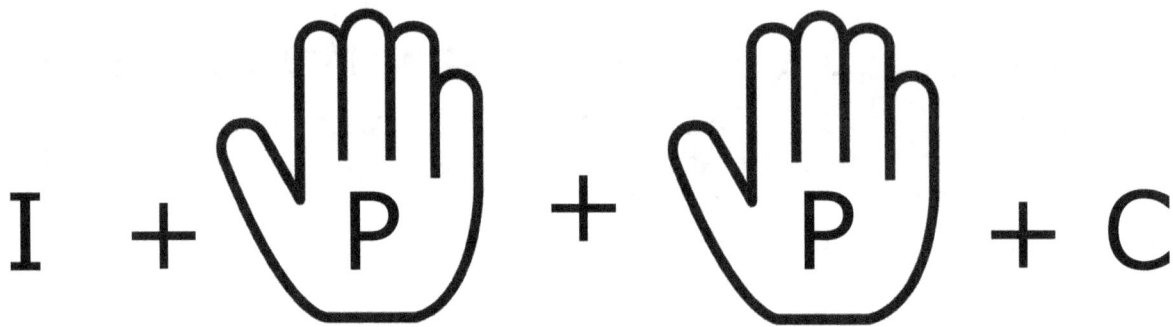

Compare & Contrast
Four Paragraph Essay
Gothic Fiction and Detective Stories

From *The Raven Remix* by Carolee Dean

Note: It may be helpful to use the High Five Writing Brainstorm Template at the end of this section for paragraphs 2 and 3.

Directions:

1. **Paragraph 1** – Write an **introduction** explaining in a general way how Poe is considered to be the father of both genres.

2. **Paragraph 2** - Use the Balloon Brainstorm to discuss similarities between Gothic Horror and Detective Stories.

3. **Paragraph 3** – Use the Balloon Brainstorm to discuss the differences between Gothic Horror and Detective Stories.

4. **Paragraph 4** – Write a **conclusion** mentioning other genres Poe is famous for like science fiction, poetry, and short stories.

5. **EDIT** – Go back through your essay to check spelling and punctuation. Make sure there are smooth transitions between the paragraphs.

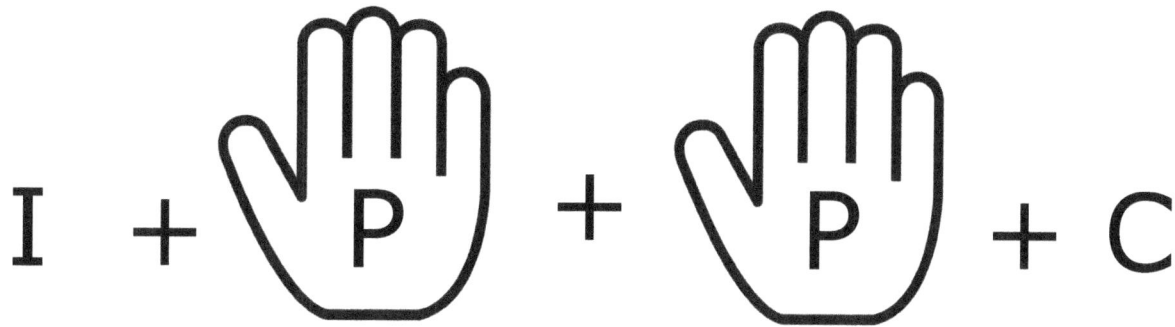

Five Paragraph Essay
Genre Gemstones
From *The Raven Remix* by Carolee Dean

Note: It may be helpful to use the High Five Writing Brainstorm Template at the end of this section for paragraphs 2, 3, and 4.

Directions:

1. **Paragraph 1** – Write an **introduction** explaining in a general way how Poe contributed to several genres. Then use the Genre Gemstones Brainstorm to write paragraphs 2, 3, and 4.

2. **Paragraph 2** - Discuss the features of detective stories in general. Then, give specific examples from "The Purloined Letter" (pages 62-63).

3. **Paragraph 3** – Discuss the features of gothic horror in general. Then, give specific examples from "The Masque of the Red Death" (pages 67-68).

4. **Paragraph 4** – Discuss the features of science fiction in general. Then, give specific examples from "The Facts in the Case of M. Valdemar" (pages 71-73).

5. **Paragraph 5** – Write a **conclusion** discussing the importance of Poe's influence on American fiction.

6. **EDIT** – Go back through your essay to check spelling and punctuation. Make sure there are smooth transitions between the paragraphs.

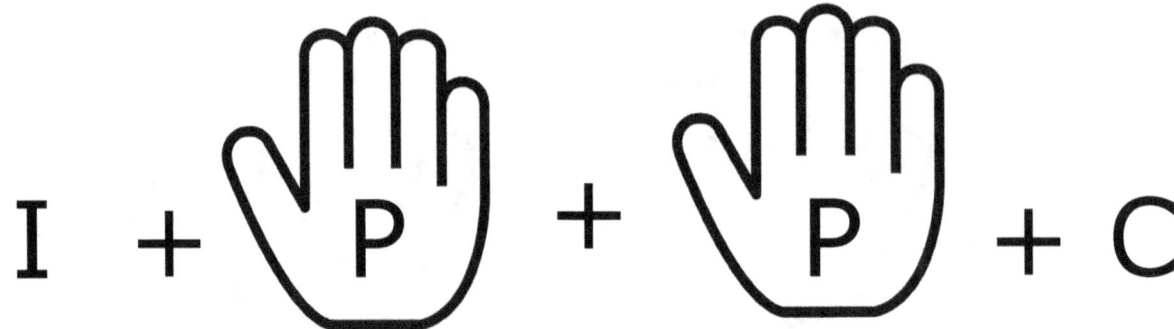

Five Paragraph Essay
Cause of Death

From The Raven Remix by Carolee Dean

Note: It may be helpful to use the High Five Writing Brainstorm Template at the end of this section for paragraphs 2, 3, and 4.

Directions:

1. **Paragraph 1** – Write an **introduction** explaining in a general way how Poe's death is a mystery that has never been solved. Then use the Cause of Death Brainstorm to write paragraphs 2, 3, and 4.

2. **Paragraph 2** - Discuss your Cause of Death theory #1 and the reasons why it makes sense. Use a citation from *The Raven Remix.*

3. **Paragraph 3** – Discuss your Cause of Death theory #2 and the reasons why it makes sense. Use a citation from *The Raven Remix.*

4. **Paragraph 4** – Discuss your Cause of Death theory #3 and the reasons why it makes sense. Use a citation from *The Raven Remix*.

5. **Paragraph 5** – Write a **conclusion** summarizing all three theories. Tell which one you think is the most likely and why.

6. **EDIT** – Go back through your essay to check spelling and punctuation. Make sure there are smooth transitions between the paragraphs.

High Five Writing Brainstorm Template

Directions: Write a paragraph based on the format below.

Note: If you are writing more than one paragraph on a topic, make a separate copy of the High Five Brainstorm for each paragraph.

Write a 1-2 sentence INTRODUCTION to your PARAGRAPH:

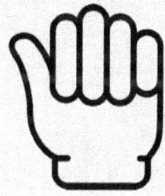

Describe three or more supporting DETAILS in three or more separate sentences.

Write a CONCLUSION for your PARAGRAPH.

High Five Paragraph Writing

Directions:

1. Use the *High Five Writing* template to brainstorm a paragraph.

2. Write the paragraph below.

3. Add transition words and signal words to make your paragraph flow. Signal words may be found in the Text Type Guide.

_____

_____

_____

_____

_____

_____

_____

_____

_____

_____

_____

CREATE

INTRODUCTION

CREATE is the highest level of Bloom's Revised Taxonomy because it requires a student to synthesize what has been learned and reorganize the information into something new. Within this domain, activities move from concrete to abstract and from factual to conceptual, then procedural, and finally metacognitive. A list of activities along this continuum is found below.

A. **Factual**: Research an animal to use in a story about **Scary Animals**.
B. **Conceptual**: Explore the concept of "parody" by writing your own funny imitation in the **Parroty Parody**.
C. **Procedural**: Follow the directions to create a **Secret Code**. Then write a private message for your friends.
D. **Metacognitive**: Consider what your view of the world would be like if you lived through all the tragedies Poe experienced. Have a class discussion about **Tragedy and Resilience** and how Poe's experiences may have influenced his writing. Consider how Poe demonstrated resilience in spite of suffering many tragedies. Then, write a reflection.

SCARY ANIMALS
based on *The Raven Remix*
by Carolee Dean

Subject: _____

Directions:
1. Poe often used animals in his stories. Pick an animal (different from the ones in *The Raven Remix)* that would be fun to use in a scary story.
2. Research the animal and make a list of fun facts about it.
3. Use the animal as a character in a scary story.

Fun Facts

Parroty Parody
based on *The Raven Remix*
by Carolee Dean

Directions:

A parody is a humorous imitation of another writer's style, characters, or subjects. "The Raven" is a story poem about a talking bird that visits a man in the middle of the night. A parrot is a bird that talks. Write a funny imitation of "The Raven" using a parrot or other annoying animal. If you prefer, choose one of Poe's other stories and create a parody. Use additional paper if needed.

Parody

Secret Codes
based on *The Raven Remix*
by Carolee Dean

Directions:

1. Practice solving the secret codes in **Alphabet Code Breakers** in the first part of this book.
2. Create a secret code below by substituting each letter of the alphabet with a different letter or symbol.
3. Write a message using your secret code. See page 33 in *The Raven Remix* for an example.
4. Skip lines so your friends can write the correct letter underneath your secret message.
5. Give your secret code to your friends. See if they can figure out your message.

Secret Code:

A=	G=	N=	T=
B=	H=	O=	U=
C=	I=	P=	V=
D=	J=	Q=	W=
E=	K=	R=	X=
F=	L=	S=	Y=
	M=		Z=

Message:

Writing with WOW Words
based on *The Raven Remix*
by Carolee Dean

Directions:

1. Follow the steps to create a vocabulary foldable.
2. After studying the words, see how many you can use in a scary short story or paragraph. Write it below.

Write your story here:

Tragedy and Resilience
based on *The Raven Remix*
by Carolee Dean

Directions:

1. Read or listen to "The Tragic Life of Poe" in *The Raven Remix*, pages 74-91.
2. Explore examples of how Poe demonstrated resilience despite tragedy.
3. Write your reflection below.

Reflection:

HOT Topics (Page 1)
The Raven Remix by Carolee Dean
(Based on Bloom's Revised Taxonomy)
https://wordtravelpress.com/

Introduction: The following list of activities is from the decodable book, *The Raven Remix: A Mashup of Poe Titles* (Level 3 from the HOT ROD Series). Activities have been designed to support Higher Order Thinking Skills and are arranged according to Bloom's Revised Taxonomy. This is just a sample to show the diversity of activities.

1. REMEMBER: Recall Details
A. **Factual**: Read *The Raven Remix* and answer the questions in the Comprehension **RACE Responses** section.
B. **Conceptual**: Complete the template for **Creature Features**. Next to each animal, write a description from the information you recall from the story.
C. **Procedural**: Using a blank piece of paper, draw a series of stick figures to show the action of *The Raven Remix*. See the directions in the ***Story Frames*** activity.
D. **Metacognitive**: Before reading the story, have students explore what they already know about Edgar Allan Poe, horror, and detective stories.

2. UNDERSTAND: Make Meaning
A. **Factual**: Copy the words and definitions from **WOW Vocabulary** onto index cards and study them. Use words to write sentences.
B. **Conceptual**: Study the **Prefix RE words for Morpho Mania**. Then play a matching game with the definitions.
C. **Procedural**: Follow the directions to create a **Vocabulary Foldable.**
D. **Metacognitive**: Study the words on the **WOW vocabulary foldable**. Predict how well you will remember the words. Then test yourself. How accurate were you in predicting your performance?

The Raven Remix by Carolee Dean
(Based on Bloom's Revised Taxonomy)
https://wordtravelpress.com/

3. APPLY: Use Information for a Task
A. **Factual**: Use the **Story Frames** stick figure drawings from 1C to retell the story or write a summary.
B. **Conceptual**: Study the Coordinating Conjunctions graphic and use it to complete the **Sentence Combining** activity.
C. **Procedural**: Use the Text Type Guide and list of Signal Words to complete the **What's My Text Type?** activity.
D. **Metacognitive**: Check your understanding as you read the story by asking yourself questions from the **PAGES strategy**. How often are you able to form a picture of what you have read? Do you use the strategy of going back to reread?

4. ANALYZE: Compare Parts to the Whole
A. **Factual**: In the **Identifying Complete Sentences** activity, *d*etermine if sentences are complete or incomplete. Then, decide if the sentence is missing a subject or a predicate.
B. **Conceptual**: Complete the **Where Things Happen** activity to find the prepositional phrases within sentences.
C. **Procedural**: Follow the directions in **Morpho Mania** for the **Structured Word Inquiry** matrices and create a list of word sums. Use the word sums to complete sentences
D. **Metacognitive**: Complete the **Clause with a Cause** activity to answer questions about why things happen in the story while working on creating dependent clauses within sentences.

5. EVALUATE: Use Criteria to Make Judgements
A. **Factual**: Use the **Cause of Death Genre Brainstorm** to list three possible causes for Poe's mysterious death.
B. **Conceptual**: List reasons to support the Cause of Death theories you chose.
C. **Procedural**: Follow the **High Five Writing Prompt** directions to write a paragraph about each Cause of Death you chose.
D. **Metacognitive**: Choose which Cause of Death makes the most sense to you and explain why you feel that way in an **IPPC essay.**

6. CREATE: Reorganize Information into Something New
A. **Factual**: Research an animal to use in **Scary Animals**.
B. **Conceptual**: Explore the concept of "parody" by writing your own funny imitation in the **Parroty Parody**.
C. **Procedural**: Follow the directions to create a **Secret Code**. Then, write a private message for your friends.
D. **Metacognitive**: Consider what your view of the world would be like if you lived through all the tragedies Poe experienced. Have a class discussion about **Tragedy and Resilience** and how Poe's experiences may have influenced his writing. Consider how Poe demonstrated resilience in spite of suffering many tragedies. Then, write a reflection.

Read more about the **HOT ROD** (**H**igher **O**rder **T**hinking through the **R**eading **o**f **D**ecodables) **Series** at https://wordtravelpress.com/

Reference:
Anderson, L.W., & Krathwohl, D. R. (Eds.). (2001). *A taxonomy for learning, teaching, and assessing: A revision of Bloom's taxonomy of educational objectives.* New York, NY: Addison Wesley Longman, Inc.

Downloads & Online Resources

Activity Pages PDF Download

Free with the Purchase of *The Raven Remix Activity Book*
The download includes:
8 Game Boards for 4-in-a-Row
32 Pages of Flash Cards for Articulation and/or Reading Practice
50+ Reproducible Activity Pages
Links to Virtual Dice

To Access the Activity Pages PDF Download,
go to www.wordtravelpress.com
Visit the Page for *The Raven Remix* (Look under Level 3 Products)
Enter the Purchaser's Code – PoeIs2C@@l

Boom™ Learning

Several virtual Boom Card decks/games are available for FREE at Boom™ Learning where you may set up a free account:
Target Word Flash Cards
Sound Tracker
Cognitive Flexibility Game

Other games found in the Activity Book have been turned into Boom™ Cards. They may be purchased and played online for a small additional fee.

Go to https://wow.boomlearning.com
Search for **Store>Word Travel Press.**

If you have any issues with access, contact info@wordtravelpress.com

References

https://affixes.org/alpha/l/-le1.html

Anderson, L.W., & Krathwohl, D. R. (Eds.). (2001). *A taxonomy for learning, teaching, and assessing: A revision of Bloom's taxonomy of educational objectives*. New York, NY: Addison Wesley Longman, Inc.

Bowers, P. (2009). *Teaching how the written word works: Using morphological problem-solving to develop students' language skills & engagement with the written word*. Ontario, Canada: Peter Bowers

Cartwright, K.B. (2023). *Executive skills and reading comprehension: A guide for educators* (Second Edition). New York, NY: Guildford Press.

Davidson, B., & Liben, D. (2019) What a knowledge-building approach looks like in the classroom. *Perspectives on Language and Literacy*, 45 (4), 31-35

Dean, C. (2021). *Story frames for teaching literacy: Enhancing student learning through the power of storytelling*. Baltimore, MD: Paul H. Brookes Publishing Co.

Duchan, J.F. (2004). The Foundational role of schemas in children's language and literacy learning. In Stone, C.A, Sillman, E.R., Ehren B.J., & Apel, K. (Eds.), *Handbook of language and literacy.* (pp. 380-397). New York: The Guilford Press

Eggleston, R. L., Marks, R. A., Sun, X., Yu, L., Zhang, K., Nickerson, N., Hu, X., Caruso, V., & Kovelman, I. (2024). Lexical morphology as a source of risk and resilience for learning to read with dyslexia: An fNIRS investigation. *Journal of Speech, Language, and Hearing Research*. https://doi.org/23814764000300140072

Eunice Kennedy Shriver National Institute of Child Health and Human Development, NIH, DHHS. (2000). Report of the National Reading Panel: Teaching Children to Read: Reports of the Subgroups (00-4754). Washington, DC: U.S. Government Printing Office.

Farrell, L.M., & Cushen-Whte, N. (2018). Structured literacy instruction. In J.R. Birsh & S. Carreker (Eds.) *Multisensory teaching of basic language skills* (4th ed., pp. 35-72). Baltimore, MD: Paul H. Brookes Publishing Co.

Green, L. B., & Klecan-Aker, J. S. (2012). Teaching story grammar components to increase oral narrative ability: A group intervention study. *Child Language Teaching and Therapy*, 28, 263–276.

Hochman, J.C. & MacDermott-Duffy, B. (2018). Composition: Evidence-based instruction. In J.R. Birsh & S. Carreker (Eds.) *Multisensory teaching of basic language skills* (4th ed., pp. 646-676 Baltimore, MD: Paul H. Brookes Publishing Co.

Kilpatrick, D.A. (2016). Equipped for reading success: A comprehensive, step-by-step program for developing phonemic awareness and fluent word recognition. Syracuse, NY: Casey & Kirsch Publishers.

Maiden, M.E., Ampuero, M.E. & Kostewicz, D.E. (2024) A Comparison of Repeated Reading and Listening While Reading to Increase Oral Reading Fluency in Children. *Education and Treatment of Children*. **47**, 51–66. https://doi.org/10.1007/s43494-024-00121-4

Moats, L.C. (2020). Speech to print: Language Essentials for Teachers. Baltimore, MD: Paul H. Brookes Publishing Co.

Nelson, N.W. (2013). Syntax development in the school-age years: implications for assessment and intervention. *Perspectives on Language and Literacy*. 39 (3), 9-15.

Paulson, L. H. (2018). Teaching phonemic awareness. In J.R. Birsh & S. Carreker (Eds.) *Multisensory teaching of basic language skills* (4th ed., pp. 205-253). Baltimore, MD: Paul H. Brookes Publishing Co.

Quinion, M. (2008). Affixes: The building blocks of English. https://affixes.org/alpha/l/-le1.html

Ramsden, Neil. Mini Matrix Maker at www.neilramsden.co.uk/spelling/matrix

Scott, C.M., & Balthazar, C. (2013). The role of complex sentence knowledge in children with reading and writing difficulties. *Perspectives on Language and Literacy*. *39* (3), 18-26.

Shanahan, T. (2015). Are you lactating? On the importance of academic language. *Perspectives on Language and Literacy, 41*(3), 14-16.

Shanahan, T. (2019). Why children should be taught to read with more challenging texts. *Perspectives on Language and Litera*cy, *45*(4), 17-23.

Stein, N., & Glenn, C. (1979). An analysis of story comprehension in elementary school children. In R. Freedle (Ed.), New directions in discourse processing (Vol. 2, pp. 53-120). Norwood, NJ: Ablex.

Tunmer, W.E., & Chapman, J.W. (2012). Does set for variability mediate the influence of vocabulary knowledge on the development of word recognition skills? *Scientific Studies of Reading*, 16(2), 122-140.

Ukrainetz, T. (1998). Stickwriting stories: A quick and easy narrative representation strategy. *Language, Speech, and Hearing in Schools*, 29, 197-206.

Vadasy, P.F., Sanders, E.A., Cartwright, K.B. (2022). Cognitive flexibility in beginning decoding and encoding. *The Journal of Education for Students Placed at Risk*.

Van Cleave, W. (2014). *Writing matters: Developing sentence skills in students of all ages (Second Edition)*. Greenville, SC: W.V.C.ED.

Wright, T.S., & Neuman, S.B. (2015). The power of content-rich vocabulary instruction. *Perspectives on Language and Literacy*, 41 (3), 25-28.

Zipke, M. (2016). The importance of flexibility of pronunciation in learning to decode: A training study in set for variability. *First Language*. 36 (1), 71-86.

HOT ROD Titles

Level 1

<u>short vowels in closed syllables and consonant blends.</u>

suffix –s, -less, -ness, -ful

About Level 1: This set includes three colorful picture books that together form the Greek Creation Myth. They are separate books but work best as a set. Book 4 is a black-and-white version of the three stories repackaged for older students. The decodable portion is the same as in Books 1-3, but Book 4 includes numerous non-fiction connections.

Level 1, Book 1: *No Gift for Man* – Zeus asks Prometheus and his brother to fill the world with living creatures. Prometheus makes man. Epimetheus creates the animals and gives them all sorts of interesting gifts, but when man comes around for his gift, there is nothing left.

Level 1, Book 2: *The Bandit* - Prometheus steals fire from Mount Olympus to give to the humans and suffers the wrath of Zeus.

Level 1, Book 3: *The Box* –Zeus gets revenge on mankind for accepting the gift of fire. The gods create Pandora, giving her many talents and charms. Then they send her to Epimetheus as a bride and give the couple a mysterious box they are told to never open.

Level 1, Book 4: *Gods and Gifts: Three Greek Myths Retold* – *No Gift for Man, The Bandit, and The Box* are told as chapters within a book for older students. It contains black-and-white illustrations. Background information about the discovery of fire, early alphabet forms, additional creation myths, and other topics are included.

Level 2

<u>digraphs, trigraphs, combinations</u>

(ng, ck, sh, th, ch, tch, qu, wh) single consonant n=/ng/ before /k/, and suffix –ing.

Hank the Tank: Animal in the Spotlight – A bear's life is saved through science and DNA.

Level 3

long vowels in open syllables, consonant-le, suffix -ed

Raven Remix – A fun mashup of popular titles by Edgar Allan Poe told in the format of the story poem "The Raven."

Levels 4 & 5

R-controlled and CVe Syllables

Cars to Carmel Popcorn: Poems About Inventions– (Coming 2025) An exploration of inventions.

Other Resources

Check out the website to find information about Activity Books, Audio Books, and Digital Games to go with each title.

Visit www.wordtravelpress.com to find the Scope and Sequence of the series.

SIGN UP for my monthly newsletter on my website to keep up with book news, articles, and free offers.

For questions or comments, write to info@wordtravelpress.com.

Watch for additional books from the HOT ROD series. Visit www.wordtravelpress.com

Happy Reading!

Carolee Dean

Notes

Notes

Notes

Notes

Notes

Notes